THE
ULTIMATE
SUCCESS SECRET

(South Florida Edition)

Become A Super Achiever - Transform Your Life and Business With Million Dollar Advice and Wisdom

Dan S. Kennedy | Andrew J. Cass

Published by: Kennedy Inner Circle, Inc.
5818 N. 7th St. #103, Phoenix, AZ 85014
Licensed for reprint to certain authorized additional publishers.

Authorized Publisher: One Lifestyle Marketing, LLC / Andrew J. Cass

DISCLAIMER AND/OR LEGAL NOTICES:

While all attempts have been made to verify information provided in this publication, neither the Authors nor the Publisher assumes any responsibility for errors,
inaccuracies or omissions. Any slights of people or organizations are unintentional.

This publication is not intended for use as a source of legal or accounting advice.
The Publisher wants to stress that the information contained herein may be subject
to varying state and/or local laws or regulations. All users are advised to retain competent counsel to determine what state and/or local laws or regulations may apply to
the user's particular business.

The purchaser or reader of this publication assumes responsibility for the use of
these materials and information. Adherence to all applicable laws and regulations,
both advertising and all other aspects of doing business in the United States or any
other jurisdiction is the sole responsibility of the purchaser or reader. The Authors
and Publisher assume no responsibility or liability whatsoever on the behalf of any
purchaser or reader of these materials.

PRINTED IN THE UNITED STATES OF AMERICA

TABLE OF CONTENTS

"A Lobster
When Left High And Dry Among
The Rocks,
Has Not Instinct And Energy Enough
To Work His Way Back To The Sea,
But Waits For The Sea To
Come To Him.
If It Does Not Come,
He Remains Where He Is And Dies,
Although The Slightest Effort
Would Enable Him To Reach The Waves,
Which Are Perhaps Within A
Yard Of Him.
The World Is Full Of Human
Lobsters:
Men Stranded On The Rocks
Of Indecision And Procrastination,
Who, Instead Of Putting
Forth Their Own Energies,
Are Waiting For Some
Grand Billow Of
Good Fortune To Set Them
Afloat."

- Dr. Orrison Swett Marden

PREFACE

By Andrew J. Cass

I'm often asked the question: "what is the *secret* to your success at such a young age?"

By the age of twenty-seven, I had earned my first million in the Investment Banking business. Before the age of thirty-five, I earned another million as an Internet Marketer. Many don't crack seven figures in even one field 'in a lifetime.' I did it in <u>two separate fields</u> before the age of thirty-five.

So I guess it's a fair question...

I'm pretty sure that growing up playing organized sports and ultimately playing college football at the NCAA Division 1 level had a big hand in it. There's something about the grueling training and the long preparation that goes into football, or any organized sport for that matter, that transfers to the business world. I'm certain though, that there are *two* very specific reasons for my success at such a young age. I'll discuss them both later in the book.

One thing I've noticed though, about myself, and all high-achievers for that matter, is that we all exhibit a *few* similar characteristics that are the most responsible for our success. However, there's really <u>only one</u> that is the most dominant. And this is <u>the one</u> that you will uncover here in the pages of "**The Ultimate Success Secret.**" I'm especially excited for you if you're an Entrepreneur, Small Business Owner or Sales Professional living in South Florida because you are about to meet even more of <u>*YOU*</u> right here in your own backyard!

In a moment, I'll introduce you to Dan Kennedy, who I had the great pleasure of co-authoring this book with. If you're not familiar, Dan is the highest paid and most sought after marketing strategist and copywriter in the country and quite possibly, one of the greatest business philosophers of our time. He's known in many circles as the *Millionaire-Maker* and the *Professor of Harsh Reality*, helping people in just about every category of business turn their ideas into fortunes. No one has influenced my success more than Dan Kennedy. In fact, it's safe to say that NO ONE has influenced the success of more Entrepreneurs, Small Business Owners, and Sales Professionals in the United States, to date, than Dan Kennedy has.

In 2008, I joined forces with Dan Kennedy and his former partner, Bill Glazer, to launch the first ever Miami Chapter of their organization, **Glazer-Kennedy Insider's Circle (GKIC***)*. GKIC is known worldwide as "The Place For Prosperity" where entrepreneurs seeking fast and dramatic growth, greater control, independence and security come together in a <u>live</u> setting each month to share timely information and "what's working today" strategies. In a short time we've become one of the fastest growing Chapters in all of North America, better known here in South Florida as **Renegade South Florida Entrepreneurs.**

Each and every month, I host a 'standing-room-only' and 'invitation-only' local Chapter Event for action-oriented, success-driven business owners and Entrepreneurs right here in in South Florida. I also lead a few high-level, specialized "private" mastermind and business coaching groups. More on that later in the book as well.

Inside the pages of this book, I'll introduce you to eight of my Chapter Members who've been invited to be co-authors of "**The Ultimate Success Secret**" along with Dan and I. As one of the hand-selected 'Dan Kennedy Certified' Business Advisors for five years now (at the time of this 2013 copyright) and Founder of the Renegade South Florida Entrepreneurs group, in partnership with the GKIC Miami Chapter, I can tell you that all of them are high-achievers in their own right with thriving businesses. Our stories and our quotes throughout the book will, no doubt, inspire you and motivate you to become more and do more. Our wisdom and advice here is invaluable. You'll find all of our contact information here as well. I encourage you to reach out and connect with us should you see fit.

Collectively, our words of wisdom within the pages of this book will have a significant impact on you and your business. There's no doubt in my mind. It's why we've teamed up to write the book – to inspire *excellence* in today's "New Economy Entrepreneur" in a society where, sadly, *excellence* in business has become somewhat scarce.

You'll hear our real life stories about overcoming obstacles, breaking through income-barriers, and achieving levels of success that most only dream of. You'll even hear a quick quote from each of us after most chapters. In fact, I'll even be so bold in saying that, by the time you're done reading this book, you'll have an entirely <u>new</u> and <u>different</u>, maybe even fresh perspective on the way you operate your business and more important, the way you operate *yourself* "in your business."

The person who handed you this book obviously cares about you and your success. Be sure to thank them for this gift. Because it *truly* is a gift. Now, sit down, relax, grab a highlighter, perhaps a cup of coffee, and read this book cover to cover. You won't regret it and I'm confident you'll thoroughly enjoy it.

Before I introduce you to the *Millionaire-Maker* himself, Dan Kennedy, allow me to be the first to invite you to join us at one of our upcoming, live Renegade South Florida Entrepreneurs / GKIC Miami Chapter events right here in South Florida. For details and to get on our Email list to be notified of the next event, visit: <u>www.NoBSMiami.com</u>

Now, Dan Kennedy...

- Andrew J. Cass

INTRODUCTION

By Dan Kennedy

What You Will Discover In This Book...

Why have I written a book with such an audacious title?

It sometimes seems like only yesterday that I was a punk kid with big ideas, adding gray to my hair to try and look a little older. I certainly do not have *that* problem now. I could stand to take some of the gray out. After a speaking engagement not long ago, my friend Lee Milteer observed that my groupies seem to be getting a lot older.

Anyway, I feel like I've stacked up enough expensive experience to justify committing some opinions about "The Ultimate Success Secret" to paper. I have gone from broke to well off; from severe struggle peaks of success in not one but three professional fields; and, along the way, I have had the good fortune of working with, hanging out with quite a number of exceptionally successful people from business, sports, entertainment.

Famous people, like Joan Rivers, who started over after her husband's suicide and her loss of her career, working for $500.00 a week on *"Hollywood Squares"*, pronounced a washed up has-been by her own agent; who re-invented her career and her life with courage and determination. And non-famous people, like Gladdie Gill, a 50+ year old school teacher living uncomplainingly with Hodgkin's disease; on her summer vacations, climbing mountains, traversing Alaska in a jeep; at home, taking care of every imaginable orphaned animal; at school, defying dullard administrators to give her students the richest imaginable learning experiences, thus earning the support of an entire community of parents and kids, and having a truly lasting impact on many lives.

I have had the privilege of working closely with a great many "from scratch" entrepreneurs who've built empires, extraordinarily successful salespeople, top executives, top speakers. I have quite literally been surrounded by and immersed in success for years. And I'm a good observer. I have not let this go to waste.

It is impossible to count the number of authors, researchers, psychologists, "motivational gurus", etc. who have been fascinated by the question of what causes some people to be successful and others to fail. We know it is not "environment", as some liberals insist; it cannot be, because out of the very worst environments come fabulously successful individuals, repetitively enough not to be passed off as aberration. Blaming external factors, and excusing a person's results because of external factors, is not going to lead anybody to the answer to this question.

In the United States, probably the most famous of authors to have attacked this question thoroughly was Napoleon Hill. His findings are summarized in his best-known book, *THINK AND GROW RICH*, a bestseller in its time, and, solely thanks to word-of-mouth, a steady seller, surviving and remaining on the fickle bookstore shelves for decades. (If, by some chance you have not read this book, you must.)

In 1917, America's first billionaire, Andrew Carnegie, set Napoleon Hill on a mission to discover the commonalities, the "principles" shared by hundreds of the most exceptional achievers of their time. Eventually, Hill arrived at thirteen such principles. Recently, management guru Stephen Covey had a blockbuster best-selling book with his "Seven Habits" of highly successful people. My speaking colleague Zig Ziglar talks about the "Ten Qualities" of successful achievers. Thirteen. Ten. Seven. Pick a number. *Well, I have the audacity to step forward and tell you that I've boiled it down to ONE.*

I changed the question to:

Is there one, single secret to success
of such overriding importance that,
if concentrated upon exclusively,
will literally change a person's entire
life experience and results?
If so, what is it?

That's right – one. I believe that I have identified the one, single, sole "secret of success" universally shared and relied on, above all other success secrets, by all extraordinarily successful individuals. And it is my contention that any person who discovers, accepts, comes to understand, and gives priority, paramount importance to this one secret can and will quickly crate unbelievable breakthroughs in his or her life.

Incidentally, my focus has been quite different than Napoleon Hill's. I have paid a lot less attention to the *thinking* of the successful, and paid a lot more attention to their *behavior*.

In this book, I have NOT come out and simply stated the ultimate secret. Frankly, I could write it down on a 3x5" card. There are several reasons why I haven't done that. First of all, it's darned hard to get $19.95 for a 3x5" card. My accountant, Snarly Stubby fingers insists that we create things we can sell for profit. (If I refuse, he swears he'll up and leave and he's the only one here with the combination to the safe where we keep the Oreos and the good Scotch.) Second, if I just tell it to you outright, in its shortest form, it lacks useful impact. I've found it is of little use to those I simply tell it to. On the other hand, those who ferret it out for themselves seem to place great value on it and get great value from it. So, I hope you can discover this secret for yourself. It is waiting for you in a number of places in this book.

I don't have any special reason to be overly mysterious, though – so, a clue. The "spark" that drove me to write this book may, in itself, be revealing. A very mundane event got me going. I had been thinking about writing a book on this particular subject for quite some time. I'd been assembling notes on it for a couple years. But there was one little incident that got me to work. On a restless night, late at night, I was thumbing through *TV GUIDE* trying to find something to watch for an hour or so when I noticed this listing:

Move: ACTION JACKSON!

That name instantly appealed to me. Who was 'Action Jackson'? How did he earn such a dramatic nickname? Well, the movie turned out to be a bad

B-picture; a run-of-the-mill cops-and-bad-guys, black exploitation film starring Carl Weathers. I would not recommend the movie. But the hero's name stuck in my mind long after the details of the movie faded. Action Jackson. *That,* I thought at the time, perfectly describes the kind of person who gets the most out of life.

Think about some of the biggest blockbuster movies of recent years. *Raiders Of The Lost Ark. Die Hard. Lethal Weapon. Batman. The Fugitive.* Think about the enduring success of the *James Bond* series. Why have these films been such enormous box office moneymakers? I think one of the answers is the dramatic juxtaposition between the movies' always-in-action adventurers and most peoples' comparative slow motion lives. The constant, the universal characteristic of such big screen heroes is their bias for action. And for an hour or two, everybody becomes an Action Jackson, living vicariously through these heroes.

What the Mediocre Majority never learns is that they do not have to settle for living vicariously through others. Anybody can be an Action Jackson --- dive headlong into the greatest adventure of all; setting and rapidly accomplishing meaningful, worthwhile goals, meeting fascinating people, visiting exciting places, living an exciting life. Even people who are above-average achievers are often guilty of seeing themselves and their own lives "smaller" than need be.

Well, I am here to tell you that those who live life "large" do share a single, Ultimate Success Secret. Through the stories, experiences and examples I've assembled for you, in this book, you can now discover that very secret and get it working for you.

- Dan Kennedy

PS: You may have purchased this book on your own, and if so, my thanks and congratulations. But it's also quite likely you received this book as a gift from one of the different business and marketing consultants, advisors, experts, coaches or GKIC members that I've worked with, or perhaps, Andrew Cass, who I've co-authored this edition with (South Florida Edition). If that's the case, you should know that the person who gave you this book as a gift is someone who embodies The Ultimate Success Secret through his or her own behavior and business. That person prizes the secret, works at living the secret, and now has invested in passing along the secret to you. If you uncover it and find it valuable, by all means, let them know.

Additional Publisher's Note: this book was first written and published in the early 1990's. Not all references to the author's life or to others in the book have been up-dated. This, in no way, invalidates the timeless message of the book, as you will see. It has been revised and updated in 2011 (1st Edition) and 2013 (2nd Edition) by Andrew J. Cass

Chapter 1
TAKE ACTION TO ESCAPE FROM PRISON

By Dan Kennedy

Have you ever been inside a real prison? A friend of mine, some years ago, served one year in the Ohio State Penitentiary, and I went to visit him frequently. I can tell you: nothing you see on TV or in the movies can even half prepare you for the shock of the real thing. I don't remember how many times I went inside and back out from behind those prison walls, but the awe, fear, disability and depression I felt never lessened, from the first time to the last. No description I could write could convey the powerlessness that came over me in that environment.

There are millions of people enduring that environment every day.

But that's a small number compared to the many millions of people who might as well be in such a prison for the little joy and satisfaction they're deriving from life. People build their own prisons, incarcerate themselves in them, and make the environments every bit as bleak, stark, depressing and debilitating as the actual penitentiary I visited in Ohio. These peoples' private prisons' block walls are constructed of complaints and resentments, the mortar from excuses, the bars forged from pessimism and procrastination.

We might say that they are locked up in "Pity Prison". Their sentence is indefinite and of their own making. They could walk out as a free man or woman at any time – *if they would just apply The Ultimate Secret Of Success.*

A Word About Heroes

As I finished the first edition of this book, the "O.J. Simpson trial" had sparked a national discussion of the relative wisdom or lack thereof of turning sports champions, entertainers, and other public celebrities into heroic role models. NBA star Charles Barkley publicly insisted, "Athletes are not role models." Unfortunately, we cannot discourage countless young people from giving them hero status. The argument against viewing people as heroes based on their proclivity for making baskets, catching passes, packing concert halls, or delivering lines in movies is a good one, as too many seem to have an equal proclivity for squandering their status, money and time on drugs, alcohol, epic sexual misbehavior and violence.

Actually, there are plenty of REAL heroes all around us. Yesterday, while killing time at the airport, I got my shoes shined. The lady doing the job, I'd guess about 35 or 36 years old, was finishing her second shift of the day with me, at 6:00 PM. Just as she was finishing, the pay phone rang; as it turns out, her teenage daughter and son are required to call her every hour to check in. She is a divorced mother of two, a high school grad, with very limited marketable job skills, doing a relatively tough job, compensated by tips so the quality of her work, her attitude, her smile are critical; she is raising two teenagers; and she is saving up money to go back to school. I had to inquire and prod to find all this out. She was not complaining, not whining, not looking for pity. A *real* hero.

After a speaking engagement in Harrisburg, Pennsylvania, I was eating dinner in the Holiday Inn restaurant. Seated several tables away, alone, was a man about my age, in a wheelchair. His hands were apparently of little use to him. He dined on a bowl of soup and a soft drink, both consumed through a straw. When the check was brought to him, he somehow produced his wallet – I didn't see how – and extracted dollar bills from it with his teeth. Here was a man saddled with obvious shoulder-to-toes physical disabilities that made a simple journey to a restaurant difficult, tiring, possibly embarrassing. No one would criticize him for dropping out and copping out. But he refused to let his handicaps imprison him. A *real* hero.

During a weekend in Las Vegas. I was leaving Caesars Palace, the man getting his car from the valet ahead of me was also in a wheelchair. He and the valet knew each other and joked together as the man hoisted himself from his wheelchair into the car. The valet then left to retrieve my car. I walked over and asked the man if he would like help getting his wheelchair into his car. "Thanks," he said, "but it's not necessary. I've been doing this for myself for 30 years and I'm thankful that I can." One-handed, he folded up the wheelchair, pulled it into the car behind him, slid across the seat, and drove off. He, too, refused to be imprisoned by his handicap. A *real* hero.

I had reason to recall these two instances and individuals recently, as my Dad had a re-occurrence of an unusual neurological condition that put him flat on his back in the hospital, unable to sit up by himself, feed himself, stand, walk or do much of anything else. His doctors did their best to convince him that he, at best, might not go beyond being helped into a wheelchair. He set goals for regaining leg strength and balance. Then for control of the upper body. Then for feeding himself. Then for dressing himself. Then he moved from hospital to long-term care facility, today's euphemism for nursing home. Then he set goals for walking. For dressing himself. And finally he got into his own car and drove himself to his apartment. Then he came back to work at the office.

I once had a blind man in a sales organization I managed. He had not been blind at birth but had lost his sight in his late teens. He worked with his wife in our business, and was an enthusiastic, effective salesperson. He told me a favorite pastime was washing and waxing his car at ten or eleven o'clock at night, in the dark; it didn't matter to him but it sure bugged his neighbors! I asked him how it was that he had avoided bitterness or self-pity. He told me: "very early on, I got to meet and talk with many other blind people and I realized that many had let their lack of sight ruin their lives. They built little prisons for themselves and locked themselves in. I was determined not to do that." A *real* hero.

Each of these individuals' lives demonstrates that positive attitudes and actions, even in the most negative of circumstances, can make a big difference.

Who Else Is Afraid Of Public S-S-S-Speaking?

Phobias are real. I've had the privileges or working with Florence Henderson on a couple of TV projects, and gotten to know her – did you know that, following the cancellation of 'The Brady Bunch', her career dried up, and her fear of flying rose up and dominated her, crippling her pursuit of career opportunities, because she could not get on an airplane? Barbara Streisand stopped doing concerts thanks to uncontrollable stage freight. Johnny Carson reportedly suffered from incredible anxiety before every show. A comedian I know well, who I won't name, has such severe stage fright he vomits before most performances.

But there's not a phobia on earth that can't be treated, conquered, controlled.

Who's afraid of speaking in public? Just about everybody! Several surveys have shown that more people fear public speaking than fear heights, snakes, serious illness, accidental death or financial failure. One survey of Fortune 1000 executives revealed speaking to groups as their #1 fear. I've been fortunate to earn a large income from speaking; as my career progressed, from a few thousand dollars to $50,000.00 and up from each speech. But if you went back to the time in my childhood when I stuttered almost uncontrollably – when I could turn one short sentence into one long s-s-s-s-s-seminar – who would have predicted this career for me?

Although the problem lessened as I matured, to this day I am still "at risk" of getting "hung up" on a word, starting to stutter, embarrassing myself, on stage, on the phone or in conversation. Was it smart to choose careers in selling and speaking? Who would have blamed me for letting this influence my career choices? I refused to do that.

My friends John and Greg Rice were imprisoned by their midget size, until a man by the name of Glenn Turner ("Dare To Be Great") got a hold of them. John and Greg can't reach all the elevator buttons without something to stand on, and Glenn Turner was the first person to tell them that even "little men" could do big things. John and Greg have become very popular motivational speakers, on the subject of 'Thinking Big!' – even though they have to climb up onto a table so the audience can see them. They achieved considerable success as real estate salesmen, even though they had to ask their customers to describe the things above sink level that they couldn't see. They've been featured on countless TV programs and in movies, built a sizable real estate investment business, and live a top quality lifestyle in sunny Florida.

For Every Handicap, Obstacle And Tragedy, There Are Two Stories.

Go ahead, name a handicap. Born and raised in a ghetto, as a latch-key kid, then surrounded by gangs, crime, drugs. A physical handicap. A crippling accident. A terrible disease. Illiteracy. Lack of education. A speech impediment. Severe phobia. Name the handicap. There are two stories to be found for every one you can think of. Story #1, unfortunately the most common, will be of people who've let that handicap imprison them. Story #2 will be of the person who has accomplished the most extraordinary things in spite of, in some cases because of, that very same handicap.

Each individual, by his or her actions, chooses which story will be theirs.

- Dan Kennedy

IMPRISONING	THE ACTION MODEL
I Can't	I Will
Resentment	Gratitude
Desire For Sympathy	Desire For Accomplishment
Dwelling On "It's Not Fair"	Search For Opportunities
Acceptance	Invention
"Maybe Tomorrow…"	Do It Now!
Withdrawal	Participation
Depression	Celebration Of Even Small Victories

'It's An Impossible Situation, But It Has Possibilities"

- Sam Goldwyn

"I think its clear that the source of most people's frustration is the 'story' they tell themselves. This was a turning point for me when I became aware of this view years ago."

- Andrew J. Cass

"Regardless of what business or industry you and your customers, clients, members or constituents are in, the one thing we all have in common is we are human beings. As such, we all want to have these things in our lives: love, security and self-esteem. To the degree you are using your business to deliver all three your business is likely flourishing.

- RJon Robins

"Surrounding myself with highly motivated people who are objective, honest and supportive is crucial in breaking past my self-imposed limits."

- Carlos Castellanos

"One small step in overcoming a limiting belief, one giant leap towards success in all areas of your life."

- Mande White

"A lot of people have this image of themselves with chains and a lock around their necks, wrists or feet. But if they looked closely they'd notice that the clasp on the lock is not fastened…. They can get out of the chains nay time they want"

- Dwight Woods

"People often choose the comfort of known misery to the discomfort of unfamiliar uncertainty. Remind yourself that your present comfort zone consists of what, at one time, was unfamiliar territory. With time and practice your comfort zone enlarges every time you confront and conquer it. Don't allow your fears to limit you."

- Christine Myers

"Having the pleasure of assisting people build businesses to create lifestyle freedom, I literally get to interview thousands of people for our team, and I can tell you that 97% of the people who think they want something different are really nothing more than slaves or prisoners of their own making – they are stuck in small thinking and small living – forever blaming others."

- Debbie Wysocki

"I think mental fear is more paralyzing than its physical equivalent. It is fear that keeps us from reaching for more or taking action. Fear of failure, fear of being embarrassed, fear of not looking good."

- John Tate

"If you are in doubt, go for it!"

- Alle van Calker

I'm here for making excuses and procrastinating...
what are you here for...?

CHAPTER 2

TAKE ACTION TO TAKE CHARGE OF EVERY ASPECT OF YOUR LIFE

By Dan Kennedy and RJon Robins

Once driving from Cincinnati, Ohio, to St. Louis, Missouri, to fight boredom, I was listening to a radio call-in show, hosted by a lady psychologist. I no longer remember her name or the name of the caller, but I certainly remember the conversation.

The caller, a woman, 40 years old, in her second marriage, spilled out a load of unhappiness and misery. Her husband didn't pay enough attention to her. Her kids were grown and no longer needed her. She was bored. Finally the host stopped her and said: "you will continue to be unhappy as long as you depend so much on others to make you happy."

I pulled the car off to the side of the road and jotted that down as a fill in the blank formula:

You Will Continue To Be Un-_____

As Long As You Depend On Others

To Make You _____

Then I wrote down a few examples:

** You will continue to be unimportant as long as you depend on others to make you feel important.

** You will continue to be un-prosperous as long as you depend on others to make you prosperous.

** You will continue to be uninspired as long as you depend on others to make you inspired.

The Miracle Formula For Taking Charge Of Every Aspect Of Your Life

Let me tell you how this Miracle Formula came to me. The very first seminar I ever attended, now more than 25 years ago, where "success concepts" were presented, was a real eye-opener for me. The speaker talked about what he called the most unpleasant success principle in the world. Well, who wants to hear about the most unpleasant anything? But I was there, so I listened. He said, repeatedly, "You are exactly where you really want to be."

Now let me tell you where I was. I had driven to the seminar in a 1960 Chevy Impala and it was not 1960. When it rained, this sad old car leaked from the top and from the bottom. The seats never dried out; they stayed musky damp in the summer, they froze and cracked in the winter. The car's frame was broken clear through, so its rear end was held up with a contraption of bailing wire, wood blocks and a turnbuckle. But there was no shame for this car. I'd paid just $25.00 for it, on payments, and it was all I could afford at the time. And the condition of the car was symbolic of a few other aspects of my life. So when that speaker said: you are exactly where you want to be – hey, I didn't like that very much.

It took me a while to stop arguing and start thinking.

Then I finally wrote down a "formula" from what I thought about, as a result of his statement. I could give it to you on the back of a matchbook – it doesn't require a whole BOOK to give you this – but don't let that diminish its importance. It is my non-humble opinion that this 'painfully arrived at formula' has truly profound importance.

Here it is:

CONTROL = RESPONSIBILITY,
RESPONSIBILITY = CONTROL

Everybody wants more control. If you take all your personal, career, financial and other goals, everything you think you want out of life, and boil all that down to a single overriding objective it is the desire for greater control. Greater control over finances, present and future. Greater control over your time and lifestyle. Greater control over your kids. Etc., Etc.

Ironically, as much as we desire greater control, we are the ones who give it all away. Every time we say…

- It's the location of our business
- It's the season
- It's the economy
- It's the supervisor who has it in for me
- It's the ay I was brought up
- It's my partner/co-worker/spouse/etc.
- It's _____

Each and every time we say an "it's the...." We really DO two things simultaneously: one, we push away a small "weight" of responsibility, and that temporarily makes us feel better, but, two, we give up an equal-sized amount of control. Whenever we deny responsibility, we give up control. Get rid of a "pound" of responsibility; lose a pound's worth of control.

The Miracle Formula In Action:
Why DOES One Person Prosper And Another Suffer?

I happen to know two people very well who are very much alike. They own two almost identical businesses. Their businesses are in neighboring, very similar towns. My observation is that they are equally skilled in the technical and administrative aspects of their business.

One, Peter E., has struggled for about seven years just to say in business. He has gained very little if any, financial ground during those years. His life is a day-to-day struggle for survival.

The other fellow, Robert L., started six years ago. His business has grown by 10% to as much as 30% each year, every year. He is now getting ready to turn it into a fortune through franchising.

When I talk with Peter E., I hear a lengthy discourse on all the outside influences that negatively affect his business. The economy, taxes, banks that won't give small business a fair shake, competition from huge corporations, and his list goes on and on and on. Every time I talk with Peter, I hear the same list. A broken record playing over and over again.

I acknowledge, by the way, that these factors do exist. I am frustrated by some of them myself. But the issue is not the existence of these factors. The issue is how much control Peter lets them have over his business. Every time Peter recites his list, he shuffles off responsibility for his situation, and that temporarily helps him feel better. But with the responsibility goes the control.

When I talk with Robert, these matters only occasionally come up. Instead, he talks excitedly about the innovative strategies he has discovered and developed to keep his business growing regardless of external influences. He exhibits healthy curiosity and quizzes me about strategies I've seen or discovered recently that might work for him. "How does that client of yours in x-business deal with this y-problem?" – he wants to know. Often, he'll say something like, "I really screwed up on this situation. Let me tell you about the base I missed and what I'm doing about it."

Robert accepts all the responsibility for his success or failure, his errors and his achievements, and because he does, he retains control.

Only 5% Exhibit Self-Reliant Behavior

A couple years ago, I did a speaking tour of all the CEO Clubs (Chief Executive Officers) in the country, for Joe Mancuso's Center For Entrepreneurial Management, and I talked with groups of corporate presidents in nearly a dozen different cities. If I heard it from one CEO, I heard it from a dozen: "It's getting harder and harder to find worthy people to promote from within."

"Why is that?" I asked.

"Only about 5% of all the people we employ consistently exhibit self-reliant behavior."

"What do you mean by 'self-reliant behavior'?"

One President answered this way: "Well, take the typists here in the office. They know that a proofreader checks their work for errors, so they rely on her rather than bothering to check their own work and consistently present her with typing done right the first time. Then we've got fifty sales reps in the field. Accounting has to constantly chase and nag every one of them to get their paperwork. My Sales Manager told me the other day that we've got one guy who we give wake-up calls to."

Another President said, "We have about 20 people in the Chicago plant. Only three or four consistently get here on time, ready to work. I figure about 5% of all the people we've ever employed, in all the different jobs, accept full responsibility for successful completion of every aspect of their jobs."

When you think through what these CEO's said, you have a simple answer to a long list of questions...

*How can I move ahead in my career?

*How can I get a better job?

*How can I start my own business?

*How can I have a better relationship?

*How can I maintain a positive outlook?

*How can I make more money?

Most people have unsaid extensions to these kinds of questions:

*How can I move ahead in my career – when others have more education than I do?... when the boss likes Steve better than me?

*How can I get a better job – when the economy's so bad?

*How can I start my own business – when I haven't got any money?

.....and so on.

The answer to these questions and many more like them is: self-reliant behavior.

How Long Will You Wait
Before Taking Charge?

The many times that I followed General Schwartzkopf on a program, I listened as he posed this rhetorical question: *if you are put in charge, when you are put in charge, what should you do? TAKE CHARGE!*

He was talking about the very essence of leadership – not waiting, not procrastinating, not looking around to copy how others did it or are doing it, not waiting for a committee to cover your butt with its recommendations; instead, stepping forward to do what needs to be done and to do what is right.

All too often, even when an individual finally gets the chance to be "in charge" that he has coveted, he accomplishes little. For years, other players on the NBA Chicago Bulls grumbled and groused about being stuck in the shadow of Michael Jordan. They coveted the chance to command that spotlight and lead the team. But when Michael Jordan retired, that spotlight searched vainly for that team's next leader. In 1994, it couldn't find one. The most logical heir-apparent embarrassed himself and his entire team in the playoffs by throwing a 'hissy fit' over not being named by the coach as the man to get the ball and try the final shot in the final seconds of a closely contested playoff game. This 'would-be leader' let his ego control his actions. Incredibly, he refused to go back in from the time out and give his best efforts to the play that had been called. You can look around and see such individuals squandering their opportunities constantly in just this way.

But I would go even farther: *why wait until you are put in charge?* Take charge anyway. The fact is: there's a leadership vacuum just about everywhere. Maybe in your home. Probably in your business or place of employment. In your industry, in your community, in your church, in your country. And I suggest this leadership vacuum offers you the opportunity you seek to change your life for the better. Let me give you a very down-to-earth example:

Mary S. was at a seminar I presented for doctors some years ago. She was there with her husband, a dentist. She pulled me aside on a break. "Could I talk to you alone for a minute?" So she and I ducked out of the meeting room, went down the hall, and found an empty meeting room to step into.

"I'm so frustrated," she told me. "There are so many things you've been talking about that we could do to build up the practice. We keep going to seminars, hearing good ideas, but my husband never gets anything new implemented. Nothing happens. The staff now knows that when he comes back from a seminar talking about new ideas, all they have to do is wait a few days and it'll all blow over. And the practice hasn't grown a bit in three years."

"What kind of things would you have him do?" I asked.

"Join the Chamber of Commerce, attend meetings and make contacts with other business people in the community," she said. "And start a mailing campaign to area business owners and executives. And put out a monthly newsletter for our past and present patients. And put together a little how-to book, something like *'How To Keep Healthy Teeth For Life.'* And, in the office, our reception area desperately needs re-decorated. The staff needs some help with handling telephone calls, especially from new patients calling in because of our yellow pages ad. And –"

"Wait a minute," I raised my hand like a traffic cop and brought her to a halt. "Mary, these all sound like inarguably good ideas to me."

"But he won't do any of them," she said sadly.

"Well, Mary," I asked, "What are *you* waiting for?"

For the first time that night, Mary was speechless. She returned to the meeting room with a particularly thoughtful look on her face.

You see, it's one thing to complain about another person's failure to pick up the ball and run with it. In this case, Mary was certainly justified in being frustrated with her husband's lack of ambition and initiative. But she'd been complaining to him and about him for three years. She'd been frustrated for three years. Obviously, that wasn't going to change anything. Her only apparent options: accept him and things exactly as-is and stop being aggravated, continue being frustrated every day of her life for the rest of her life, divorce him and leave, or pick up the ball and do some running of her own.

Most would choose one of the first two options. Henry Thoreau observed "Most men (and women) lead lives of quiet desperation."

About a year later, Mary S. appeared at another of my many seminars for doctors. Again she cornered me on a break, apart from her husband. "I want to tell you," she began, "that I was very angry with you and the way you answered me that night. I wanted some sympathy. And I wanted you to go have a tough talk with my husband. But I sure didn't want you to challenge *me*."

"Should I apologize?" I asked.

"Hardly," she answered. "Let me tell you about my new life." Mary no longer worked in the office as a dental assistant. Instead she had hired her replacement, then appointed herself 'Director Of Marketing.' She joined the Chamber of Commerce, a businesswomen's club, a Toastmasters group, and enrolled in a Dale Carnegie class. She assembled a book – *"Secrets Of A Healthy Smile For Life"* – and she began speaking to groups of school children, PTA meetings, civic groups, everywhere she could on behalf of the practice. She put together a practice newsletter, assigned writing tasks to other staff members and occasionally even to patients, got it done, published and out every month. She designed a new 'Family Plan' to promote to the practice's patients. She created and promoted 'Patient Appreciation Weeks.'

In five months, the practice doubled. Although shocked at first, her husband adapted to her new role and new interests. And he was kept pretty busy just handling the new patient flow anyway.

"Now I work just three or four hours a day, doing all the marketing and promotion for the practice – I'm our 'Mrs. Outside', he's our 'Mr. Inside', and I've even got time for my new venture, creating and publishing health-related coloring books for kids, distributed through dentists nationwide. *I'm not waiting anymore,"* she concluded.

Now, what are <u>you</u> waiting for?

- Dan Kennedy

"Are you pleased

with your present

place

in the world?

If your answer is *yes,*

what's your next port of

call?

If your answer is *no,*

what are you going to do

about it?

Earl Nightingale
From: Earl Nightingale's
Greatest Discovery
Published by Dodd/Mead

In the words of RJon Robins...

At the end of every day, in order for any business to be successful every entrepreneur knows it must create some sort of value for its customers, clients, patients, members, constituents, or whatever label you put on the people who do business with you.

Therefore if we are to be in business successfully, we must accept responsibility for being sure the business delivers value; even if the business you're accepting responsibility for isn't technically *your* business.

Because regardless what business, industry or profession you're in, the one thing we all have in common is that we're human beings. As such, we're all fundamentally motivated by the same three things.

Even if your customers are companies, it's still a human being or a group of human beings who make the decisions and choose whether or not to do business with you. For example, at the time of this writing I'm currently on a national speaking tour being sponsored by Microsoft, an absolutely mind-bogglingly-huge multinational conglomerate. But it's still just a small group of individuals at Microsoft with whom my team and I interface in order to make this happen.

Now the thing to understand about human beings...no matter what company they work for, which industry they're in or how many letters follow their name... we each want to have the same three things in our lives: Love, Security & Self-Esteem.

To the degree you are using your business as a vehicle to <u>give</u> all three of these to your customers, clients etc., that's likely where your business is flourishing.

To the degree you're trying to get love, security and/or self-esteem <u>from</u> your business, its customers, clients, vendors or employees, that's surely where your business has its most pressing problems and the greatest opportunity for immediate improvement.

There may be an exception to this simple rule. But I believe you'll have a happier life and a more successful business just as quickly as you focus on applying this rule rather than wasting time looking for an exception; if an exception can even ever be found.

Dan talks about the relationship between taking responsibility and gaining control. He says the more control we have, the more income, freedom etc. we can enjoy. And I can attest to the accuracy of this cause-effect relationship in my own life and business.

I used to aspire to have control in my business for the sake of having control. I suppose you could say I was a control freak. Which in my industry, that's too-often accepted as an excuse. Usually in the form of a badge of false honor and used as an excuse to avoid having to put in the work necessary to live up to our potential. Sometimes it's made by lawyers who simply misunderstand the secret power of control Dan talks about in this chapter.

You see, effects all have causes. We even have a hundred years of case law to support this fact. But control is both a cause and an effect. It's a natural effect when you're delivering value. It's also the cause of success.

I tell members of my solo & small law firm coaching groups that "Happy Lawyers Make More Money". Many join our various coaching programs seeking better business management and marketing systems, administrative processes, proven law office management procedures and other "best practices" about the business of starting, marketing & managing a law firm that hardly any law schools teach. And I congratulate each and every one of them for accepting responsibility for learning these critical skills of success.

What they soon learn though, is the same thing I learned the hard way but only after wasting too many years of my life and career: Unless the control is used as a cause -- that is, unless control over a law firm is used to cause the firm to deliver more value to prospective, current and even former clients, referral sources and staff -- the control will be fleeting or illusory.

Because control achieved for the sake of control eventually grows dull. Instead it must be sharpened by use to deliver value.

Analyzing the answers to three simple questions can help you get a handle on this about any business:

Love – Do your clients, customers, etc. feel that they are important-to, and appreciated-by you and your team?

Security – Does their relationship with you and your company, cause your clients and customers to be more-likely to achieve their own goals in life?

Self-Esteem – Do your clients and customers feel better about themselves for having chosen to do business with you and your company?

To the extent, and nearly as quickly as any entrepreneur accepts responsibility for being sure the processes, procedures, products and services of their business deliver love, security and self-esteem to clients, those entrepreneurs will experience an easier time selling, with less price resistance, more repeat & referral business, more cooperative clients or customers and a more cheerful & collaborative staff.

I encourage you to make up your mind right now and take responsibility for finding ways to use your business as a vehicle to give love, security and self-esteem. You will surely be rewarded with more control in both your business and in the rest of your life too.

A favorite quote of mine from Ayn Rand:

"Money demands that you sell, not your weakness to men's stupidity, but your talent to their reason."

- RJon Robins

RJon is the founder of How To Manage A Small Law Firm.com the leading international management & marketing coaching program for owners of high-performance solo & single shareholder small law firms. RJon practices what he preaches (and what Dan preaches) about the efficacy of education-based marketing which is why he offers a variety of FREE resources to help lawyers including: "The 6 Most Common, Costly & Frustrating Mistakes Most Lawyers Make When Starting A Law Firm"; "A Simple System For How To Manage A Law Firm IOLTA Trust Account That Won't Make You Feel Like A Schmuck"; "The Professional, Ethical & Profitable Law Firm Management Manual They SHOULD Have Given All Of Us In Law School". All of these and more FREE resources to help you are available today at: www.HowToManageASmallLawFirm.com

---

"I've believed for some time now that the word 'waiting' is one of the most crippling words in the English language."

- Andrew J. Cass

"The question isn't who is going to let me; it's who is going to stop me." – Ayn Rand (Often repeated by RJon Robins)

- RJon Robins

"The attention generated by having created 'BALDO', the first nationally syndicated Latino Family comic strip was quite uncomfortable for me. But making the decision to embrace it has resulted in priceless opportunities and gratifying relationships."

- Carlos Castellanos

"Since taking 100% responsibility for my life, so many new possibilities have opened up. I think it's fun to play with this ability to choose my own adventure in life."

- Mande White

"One you realize that you can control only yourself, your actions, reactions, etc. you develop the ability to respond to different situations in your live… You develop RESPONSE-ABILITY!

- Dwight Woods

"Be it…Own it…Live it!

- Christine Myers

"Dan's simple formula 'Control = Responsibility; Responsibility = Control' should be on every entrepreneur's wall."

- Debbie Wysocki

"It seems people often wait for a set of perfect conditions to be there before taking action… 'As soon as this project is completed'… 'As soon as I have more money'… 'As soon as I have spare time.' That perfect set of conditions will never occur."

- John Tate

"Don't try, just do it!"

- Alle van Calker

CHAPTER 3

TAKE ACTION TO GET THE KNOW-HOW YOU NEED

By Dan Kennedy and Carlos Castellanos

Not knowing how to do something has never stopped me from setting out to do it, and I've become convinced that anybody can become competent, even expert, at just about anything; there are books, cassettes, courses, classes, teachers, mentors, newsletters, associations, an absolute abundance of information linked to virtually any and every skill or ability or occupation you can think of. A whole lot of it is readily available, free. More at very modest cost. Some, pricey.

I am frequently amazed and dismayed at the people who seek me out and ask questions that evidence they haven't even done an ounce of homework or research on their own. Today, a business owner came to me after I finished delivering a speech on advertising and marketing, handed me the advertising flyer he'd prepared and invested his hard-earned money in having printed and distributed, and said, "What do you think?"

I had a few questions of my own. "Before you put this together," I said, "what books did you go and get about writing advertising headlines? About advertising in general" And I could have asked a dozen more questions along these same lines. The answers were, frankly, pitiful. Non-existent. He had done nothing, nada, zero to prepare himself for the task of putting together effective advertising flyers. When you look at this objectively, from the outside in, it's pretty obvious that this is stupid behavior. And quite bluntly, if you insist on behaving stupidly, you do not deserve positive results.

Ignorance about any particular subject is forgivable and, fortunately, fixable. Stupidity is another story altogether.

The Serious Student At Work

When I became earnest about using more humor in my speeches and seminars, and getting good at using it, for example, I found no shortage of assistance out there. Beyond simply observing and analyzing great humorists and comedians, I found plenty of books on the subject, Esar's *Comic Encyclopedia,* videos, seminars, newsletters, and audiocassette courses. I learned "timing" from listening to a fantastic humorous speaker, Dr. Charles Jarvis, from comedian Shelley Berman, and others, over and over and over again. I read all the classic masters – Benchley, Thurber, I read all the contemporary humorists, I read everything Steve Allen ever wrote, I found 'old' comedy records, I subscribed to humor services like Orbens. I became a very serious student of humor.

Gradually I transitioned from picking and telling jokes to creating original material, from jokes to humorous stories. I did a whole lot of homework.

When I got involved in teaching advertising, marketing and sales to doctors of chiropractic, I became a serious student of the chiropractic profession. I subscribed to the profession's journals, I got and read books, I visited offices, I went to seminars, I asked questions of doctors. In a few months, I knew enough and sounded so much like a chiropractor that we had to continually correct doctors who called me "Dr. Kennedy" and convinced themselves I was one of them. To this day, I'll be walking through a hotel lobby, airport, mall and have a chiropractor yell out, "hello Dr. Kennedy!" And, although I would never give an adjustment, I can do a decent exam, a good report of findings, I can sell people on chiropractic better than most chiropractors, and I could operate a practice. I could go to a convention and easily pass myself off as a doctor if I chose to. I'll bet I could go to an office and get myself hired as an associate doctor.

Some years back, I worked closely with a client in the retail theft control business. His company dealt with employee and deliveryman theft in supermarkets, convenience stores and drug stores (where it is an immense problem). Then, I subscribed to all the trade journals of the supermarket, convenience store and drug store industry, and assembled articles about theft from several years of back issues. I read what books I could find on the subject. I studied my client's materials. I learned the language of retail finance. To this day, I can walk into any such store or restaurant and, in 5 minutes, tell you whether or not the employees are stealing and, if so, show you the "hidden evidence" that proves it. And I could give a seminar to retailers on the subject and no one would question my status as an expert.

I'm not bragging. I'm just pointing out that it isn't very difficult to quickly acquire expertise in a given area, if that's what you want to do. But it's amazing to me the number of people who just never bother.

When I worked with the chiropractors, I used to ask groups for a show of hands – how many had really studied even one book or course on how to sell. In most groups, less than half; yet everyday, their incomes depend on their effectiveness at selling...selling the public and new prospective patients on chiropractic, selling new patients their recommendations and their fees. They're not alone. Just about every business or occupation is a composite of several different types of expertise, but most people master one and are content being an amateur in the others.

If not knowing about something stands between you and what you want to accomplish, get busy and go get that know-how. If really is that simple.

The 7 Ways To Get Smarter About
Virtually any Subject – FAST

1. Find and read at least a year's back issues of the related trade or specialty magazines.

Every business, industry, occupation, vocation, hobby or special interest – from cooking to computer programming, from ostrich farming to searching for lost gold mines, from long-haul truck driving to golfing, from writing to woodworking, from Astrology to zoology – has one, in most cases, several magazines all its own. In these magazines, the experts write articles, are interviewed and profiled, how-to secrets are revealed, advertisers promote their wares.

2. Answer a lot of the ads you find in these magazines.

Let all those advertisers try to sell you their products and services. Soon, you'll be deluged with information. All coming to you, free.

3. Find the top experts, most successful people and most celebrated people in the field.

Such people have probably written books, recorded audiocassettes, they may sell such products, seminars or consulting, and/or they may even be approachable just to talk with or visit with free. Seek out the best and the brightest and find out how you can best turn their experience into your knowledge. Surprisingly, even in competitive fields, these outspoken experts and super achievers exist.

Some years back, I worked with a chiropractor who started his own practice immediately after school. Almost immediately. First, armed with a list he had painstakingly compiled of 50 of the most successful, most respected chiropractors in the country, he got in his car and drove across country, north, south, east and west, going to each of their offices, asking if he could observe, take the doctor to lunch or dinner and pick his brain, visit with the staff, and so on. Forty-nine of the fifty were gracious, generous, encouraging and helpful. He arrived home with what he called 'A Master Practice-Building Plan From The Masters Of The Profession'. He had great confidence in this plan. He implemented it with natural enthusiasm and positive expectation. And he built a record-breaking practice in short order.

If I were to start in a brand new business today, I would follow his example.

4. Find the books written by "the OLD masters."

Just about every field has "old masters", whose works are hard to find or even out of print, who many ignore as passed by time and no longer important. They're wrong.

In the selling field, every salesperson should read books by Frank Bettger, Red Motley, Robert Trailins, to name a few, from the 1950's, the 1940's, and earlier if you can find them. Robert Trailins' "old book", *DYNAMIC SELLING,* published by Prentice-Hall a long time ago, to be found only in libraries or used bookstores, offers better advice on crafting powerful appointment-getting presentations than any book, seminar or course I'm aware of.

In direct-response advertising and copywriting, today's top pros, like my friends Gary Halbert and Ted Nicholas, and I, constantly refer novices to the works of the "old masters," Robert Collier, Claude Hopkins, Victor Schwab and others, dating back to the 1930's.

I would add, of course, the suggestion that you read MY books, and I'm reluctant to say it, but I'm reaching the "old master" status. For selling, read my *NO B.S. SALES SUCCESS IN THE NEW ECONOMY* book. For marketing, read *NO B.S. DIRECT MARKETING FOR NON-DIRECT MARKETING BUSINESSES,* as well as *THE ULTIMATE MARKETING PLAN* and *THE ULTIMATE SALES LETTER.* For entrepreneurship, read *NO B.S. BUSINESS SUCCESS IN THE NEW ECONOMY* and *NO B.S. WEALTH ATTRACTION IN THE NEW ECONOMY.* They're all readily available at bookstores, BN.com, amazon.com, or you can get free information about them at www.NoBSBooks.com.

5. Join trade associations or clubs.

The "learning curve shortcuts" available through trade association membership and attending association conventions and workshops is remarkable. The opportunity to make dozens and dozens of important and beneficial contacts is even greater.

Most associations have archives of tapes from past years' conventions and workshops, so you can "attend" two, five, even ten years of past events as if a time machine was at your disposal.

Many national associations have state, regional or city "chapters" with easily accessible meetings and seminars, usually all at very modest costs. If you are interested in writing, for example, The National Writers Club has Chapters in most states. If you are interested in speaking, the National Speakers Association has Chapters in many cities.

At Glazer-Kennedy Insider's Circle (GKIC), we now have local chapters and private coaching groups throughout North America. You can join your local group right here in South Florida, known as Renegade South Florida Entrepreneurs, run by Andrew J. Cass, the GKIC Certified Independent Business Advisor (IBA), and co-author of this book. For more information visit: www.NoBSMiami.com

6. Take a class, workshop or seminar.

Community colleges are getting more and more progressive and competitive in their class offerings and their use of bona fide, real world experts as instructors. The seminar organization, The Learning Annex, with operations in many major cities, offers the most diverse assortment of classes I've ever seen – everything from how to start an import/export business to how to become a belly dancer or how to strip like a pro to how to buy and sell antiques.

Somewhere, there's somebody giving a class, workshop or seminar on just about any subject you might imagine. (There is, for example, a bona fide expert who takes a few people at a time fishing for a week, at a hefty

$5,000.00 a pop, and teaches them "how fish think" so that they can more easily catch more fish. Laugh if you will, but he is for real, and was the subject of a very successful TV infomercial, *"Outdoor Challenge",* hosted by Curt Gowdy, produced by my friend Pam Daily, for which I wrote the commercials.

My friend Jerry Patterson has hundreds of loyal, happy students at his periodic 'casino gaming conventions', where he teaches his blackjack methods.)

One great source of information about top quality courses, seminars and conferences, is at: www.GKICResourcesMiami.com

7. <u>Do your homework.</u>

The good old-fashioned public library is a place to start. Most major city libraries have self-serve, easy to use computer systems, so you can plug in any topic and find all the books, articles and other resources related to it. There is a master directory published

for every imaginable subject, and if you can't find one in your area of interest, there is a 'Directory Of Directories' to help you.

Or you could *Google* it.

- Dan Kennedy

In the words of Carlos Castellanos...

It's funny how sometimes the most seemingly inconsequential experience, or action, can set off a ripple effect that sets you on a journey of growth and discovery, defining your life, your purpose.

I remember rushing home one afternoon after school to watch an episode of *Bewitched*. In this particular episode what caught my attention, despite all the magic and shenanigans that were central to the show, was the image of Darrin Stephens sitting behind a large wooden drawing table in his home office working on ad campaigns and drawing cartoon characters. For some reason, that image stuck in my head; time seemed to freeze. In that moment, I decided that's what I wanted to do. Like Darrin Stephens, I wanted to sit behind a large wooden drafting table from a home office and draw. I was in second grade. Little did I know, I created an image in my mind so powerful, it literally propelled me down a path of taking action and acquiring the knowledge necessary to create that scenario in my life.

Not having art classes available to me throughout my teen years, I sought out ways to develop my drawing skills by reading everything I could related to drawing. I started collecting and studying the iconic artists in Mad Magazine and Marvel comic books. I practiced and drew constantly. Through my school years I was labeled "class artist" by friends and peers and had developed my skills substantially considering I was self-taught.

The information was out there, and being a curious kid, I made it my mission to find it. That's not to suggest I was special in any way. We all have something that we excel at, mostly because we dedicate time and effort to it. Kids are extremely curious by nature and very creative in getting what they want. They approach problem solving as a fun, creative game without all the hang-ups. Heck, my kids prove this daily.

As adults however, I find that we allow excuses to get in the way of getting a lot of what we want simply because we don't know something. We develop this idea that if we were meant to do or be a particular thing, we would already have the knowledge to do it,

or at the very least, it would somehow come easier to us. We pigeonhole ourselves into what we can and cannot do. Can or cannot have. It keeps us thinking small, feeling small, and thinking wrong.

Mentoring - A Shortcut to Success

In 1982, while still in college as a first-year commercial art major, I was fortunate enough to have an illustration instructor who recognized my dedication and took an active interest in my work. He offered to teach me the basics of getting started in freelancing for a class grade. So while my fellow classmates were being graded on completing class projects, I was out making cold calls, hustling to show my portfolio and meeting with art directors trying to land some paying gigs.

Without realizing it at the time, he became my first business mentor. I began my freelance career as an illustrator without having a clue about business, how to find business, or even what to charge. I was clueless. Nonetheless, within several months under his guidance, I had enough clients to keep me busy. I was making more money than I had ever made before, doing what I used to get in trouble for doing in the back of my seventh-grade math class. I was getting paid to draw.

That was a valuable lesson for me. Still, there have been times when I've forgotten what got me to the dance. A few times over the years (actually more times than I'd care to recall), I struggled needlessly in my business simply because I didn't have the information I needed to accomplish a goal or achieve an outcome I wanted. I was slothing through, trying to figure stuff out on my own, frustrated with meager results, and wasting time month after month trying to reinvent the wheel. Like so many freelancers and solo-preneurs, I'm wired to going it alone. Doing everything myself. Only to later remember there is an easier way. As my wife can attest, I can be pretty dense sometimes. So now I've continued to develop my skills and knowledge, investing heavily in educational resources, workshops, seminars, conferences, and coaching necessary to not only survive as a professional artist, but to grow, expand, and create new opportunities for myself.

My association with the Renegade South Florida Entrepreneurs / GKIC Miami Chapter has been instrumental in my success.

Most artists wouldn't consider themselves entrepreneurs. But I've come to believe artists and entrepreneurs are very similar in nature. We're deeply passionate, driven, focused, and creative. We dream big and can clearly see the outcome of what we want to create. We're the dreamers in our society.

Making Comic History

In 1998, looking for an opportunity to produce more personal work, I partnered up with my friend Hector Cantú. We started developing the "Baldo" comic strip with the hope of getting it picked up by a top syndicate. The premise of the strip was a simple one: the exploits of a day-dreaming, Hispanic-American teen and his family, living and balancing dual cultures in the US. From a personal standpoint, it gave us the opportunity to reflect on plenty of funny experiences from our youth, but also let us explore more topical events in the quickly growing Hispanic community that the mainstream media was slow to address or disinterested in covering.

To our surprise, it received an overwhelmingly positive response from syndicates. In April of 2000, "Baldo" was picked up by Universal Press Syndicate and launched nationally to almost 100 newspapers, making it Universal's third most successful launch in its 30-year history, at the time! "Baldo" was the first Latino family to appear in the funny pages.

With the launch came a wave of national media attention. Multiple opportunities arose to do interviews on local and national radio

stations, newspapers, magazines, and TV news networks, such as CNN and Univision. I've been invited to serve on several expert panels in a wide range of conferences ranging from Hispanic Health to Advertising. We even produced "Baldo" as an animated TV show with a major television network.

Being fairly introverted as most artists are, I did the uncomfortable. I left the safety of my studio. I learned to field questions from the media and overcome my fear of public speaking. Again, I sought out the coaching and support I needed most to help me capitalize on the new opportunities. All this made possible through the steady growth of confidence gained from consciously seeking out and developing myself through newly acquired skills and knowledge. Some free, some bought.

Surround Yourself with the Right Support

When I decided to start producing my work digitally in 1998, I was a complete computer newbie. I was clueless. Faced with the option of buying a Mac or a PC, I chose Mac. Not because it was better (I couldn't tell you to this day which is better). Truth is, I didn't care. The reason I chose the Mac is simple: SUPPORT. Many of my friends and clients were already working on Macs. I had a knowledgeable support network I could call on to learn from and to help me troubleshoot problems, fast.

Investing time and resources in getting the knowledge you need is an investment in yourself. Learning from others, going to live events, and investing in myself as an illustrator has opened the door to me working and meeting some incredibly inspiring and successful people in many industries including Internet Marketing experts Mike Koenigs, Andrew J. Cass, Maritza Parra, and Bill Glazer.

Pursuing Your Passion

I have the privilege of being invited to appear and speak at countless schools and libraries, encouraging children and adults of all ages to be confident in expressing their creative vision and sharing their unique voice. It's never been easier to create a respectable lifestyle as an artist doing the work that most inspires you. We live in an economy that is increasingly placing more value on an individual's ability to be unique and original. Access to your audience has limited barriers, allowing you to connect on a much deeper level while solving problems for clients or inspiring a movement.

Mentoring and coaching others has been one of the most rewarding experiences of my career. Now I coach and mentor other freelance artists on how to build more emotionally satisfying careers so they too can achieve the level of success and lifestyle they desire, doing the meaningful, creative, fulfilling work they love most and help them share it with the world.

My biggest growth as an artist and entrepreneur has come from choosing to stop struggling and going it alone, discover the steps, mindset, or systems others before me have already solved, and make the commitment to acquire that knowledge no matter what. Surround yourself with the people who can supply you with the know-how, encouragement, and accountability you need, and you will grow yourself into opportunities you can't even imagine.

- Carlos Castellanos

Carlos is an award winning illustrator/syndicated cartoonist and entrepreneur. He is the co-creator and artist behind the popular nationally syndicated newspaper comic strip 'BALDO', the most widely distributed Latino family comic strip appearing in over 250 daily and Sunday newspapers and read by millions nation wide.

Artists: Get Free Instant Access to my *"Make Over 100k Per Year as an Artist"* audio presentation when you visit: www.DrawnBySuccess.com/bonus

---

"There no shortage of information nowadays which means there's no shortage of opportunity, therefore I don't think anyone gets to complain about not getting ahead."

- Andrew J. Cass

"Just about anyone can turn him or herself into one of the leading authorities in most practice areas in 12 months or less by following just the steps outlined in this chapter."

- RJon Robins

"Beyond my artistic skills and creativity, the dominant factor to much of my success has come from learning to identify my client needs. What I do, how I do it and whom I do it for. Being a good artist is simply not enough."

- Carlos Castellanos

"This is definitely a success secret I live by. At least 20% of my time is spent in books or training programs that help me expand my mind to new possibilities and ways of thinking, being & doing."

- Mande White

"Everyone talks a good game about how much they want to achieve, how good they want to be until they discover the amount of work involved in getting from Point A to Point B."

- Dwight Woods

"Leaders are Readers"

- Christine Myers

"Everyone has different learning styles. However, if you are reading this book and searching for success, YOU MUST BE A LIFE LONG STUDENT. I am amazed at how much my brain absorbs. We have so many resources… use them!"

- Debbie Wysocki

"Immediately out of college, my consulting firm employer billed me at a seemingly ridiculous $200/hr. So that I didn't embarrass my firm and myself, I needed to provide significant value to clients. Often, I was able to make them very happy simply by being just one step ahead of them in my knowledge of a topic or task."

- John Tate

"Stay up to date in your field of business and apply what you learn. If you don't use it, you'll lose it, and if you rest, it will rust."

- Alle van Calker

CHAPTER 4

REVERSING THE FORMULA

By Andrew J. Cass

I'm too often amazed at how few people seek knowledge, new skills, and expertise nowadays. It's as if they think success and wealth is somehow going to land on them like rain falling out of the sky. Society has many believing that if you go to school and gets a degree or a certification of some kind, suddenly you will no longer need to acquire *new* knowledge and *new* skills. As if you're now *done*. That couldn't be further from the truth.

We're now in the Information Age yet, oddly, many people seem to be seeking less information today about "skill improvement" even though there is more of it than ever before. How could this be?

As the late, great Jim Rohn always said: "Formal education will make you a living, self education will make you a fortune."

Is it any wonder why so few are truly successful and/or wealthy today?

I remember as a kid growing up just outside of Boston, all I wanted to do was play football. I decided to attend one the top football high schools in the entire state of Massachusetts (Xaverian Brothers High School). The problem was, I was a bit too small and not that fast (actually, way too small and not fast at all). I was cut from the freshman football team and had to play football that year with the 8th graders. It was embarrassing for me, to say the least. That would have been the end for most. For me, it became the beginning...

I went out an acquired all the knowledge I could on how to get bigger, stronger, and faster so I could compete and play football for this high school. I forced myself into a situation that was clearly over my head and way out of my comfort zone. I read the books, bought the trainings, and spent many hours in the gym. I was right back on the field my sophomore year to play on the junior varsity team. Still, not that fast and not that good, but back.

Throughout high school, I gradually got bigger, stronger, and faster. Not by chance. Not by luck. By the time I was a senior I was the starting Wide Receiver and I led the team in touchdowns that year. I was also the only player that year to go on to play football at a NCAA Division 1 University, Hofstra University, in New York. In fact, I had acquired so much knowledge and skill in the area of training and fitness that by the time I was through with college, I had become a Certified Personal Trainer. I even did some strength and conditioning work for the Hofstra Lacrosse team, consistently one of the top ranked Lacrosse programs in the nation.

Had I decided _not_ to seek the knowledge, the resources, and put in the hard work to get better, I might have given up and gone on to something else. Too many people nowadays to easily just *"go onto something else"* as if success is a menu with items to carelessly choose from at will. There's no doubt this experience was a turning point in my life and I attribute much of my success in business to it. In fact, Personal Training actually became my very first business at the age of 19 as a result of all the training knowledge I had acquired. And a very successful one at that. I guess you could say I turned my knowledge into money...

What many don't realize is that professional football players actually spend far more time in the classroom and the film room studying than they do on the field. Having played the sport at the NCAA Division 1 level, I can tell you first hand that the ratio of on-the-field *doing* vs. off-the-field *studying* is about 50% / 50%. In the National Football League, where players are paid many millions of dollars per year, that ratio is about 80% / 20%. And that 80% I might add, is NOT on-the-field, but in the class room studying film of their opponents along with structuring new plays and game plans for the week ahead.

It's counter-intuitive, I know. But so is success. It's never obvious.

Most don't know this, or believe me when I tell them, but I've been there. Many think football players just go out and run around tackling each other on Sundays. That couldn't be further from the truth. They actually study their craft more than many doctors do. They are true *specialists*. And their bank accounts reflect it. I'll bet you can find this same behavior present in just about every super-successful, high-achieving business owner or Entrepreneur...

How about you? What's your ratio? Do you know?

The price to pay for NOT acquiring *new*, additional knowledge and expertise today is far greater than the price of acquiring the knowledge.

Most have it the other way around though, which is why most struggle, and will continue to struggle, until they reverse this simple, yet profound, formula.

I'll leave you with a favorite quote of mine: *"school is never out for the Pro."*

- Andrew J. Cass

CHAPTER 5

TAKE ACTION TO SHED EXCESS BAGGAGE AND DISCOVER NEW CAPABILITIES

By Dan Kennedy and Mande White

In a novel *"Line Of Duty"*, author Michael Grant has one of his characters deliver this: *"A guy I fish with once told me a funny story. He'd just bought an anchor, and as he went forward to tie it to the anchor line, he slipped and fell overboard. Suddenly, he's sitting on the bottom of the lake in fifteen feet of water, cradling his brand new anchor. He didn't want to let go, but he was running out of breath. Realizing his choice was drowning or losing the anchor, he reluctantly let go and swam to the surface."* The character in the novel, a police detective, went on to say: *"The Job has been my anchor and I've been holding on to it for 23 years. I don't want to let go either, but I've run out of breath."*

Most people can be caught holding onto prized anchors.

Another way to look at it is in terms of roles. A person gets so used to a role, so comfortable in that role that, even though unhappy, the fear and trauma of stepping outside the role feels worse than the pain of continuing in it. Such roles include: The Victim *(why me – it's so unfair)*, The Martyr *(I gave up everything for you)*, The Last Angry Man *(I'm mad as hell at everybody and everything – but I will keep taking it)*, The Misunderstood Genius, and so on.

So much of our current thoughts and actions have their basis in child-hood. My aversion to having a large house with a yard to care

for is the direct result of growing up in over-large homes where there was always some damned thing in need of repair or cleaning or replace-ment, some project to be done or, worse, some disaster to be battled – like, in our second house, a basement that flooded every spring to such a degree that the neighborhood's animals lined up two by two outside. And growing up with yards always in need of mowing or weeding (until I discovered that a hungry Shetland pony on a tether made lawn mowers obsolete). Anyway, I am emotionally averse to all that. Of course, that's obvious. No need for years of therapy to figure that out. And it's not particularly important. But it is only one of, who knows how many, examples of today's thoughts, atti-tudes, likes, dislikes, fears, ideas and behaviors firmly rooted in childhood programming that has never been challenged or even re-considered.

In cases where this does no harm, or even helps, I suppose there's no need to tinker with it. But what about the baggage that does burden, the anchor that does drown, the past programming that does limit? It is plain as can be that people are controlled – yes, controlled – throughout their adult lives by limits that were set and by behaviors that were prescribed early on, then never challenged.

<u>If you are not achieving the results you tell yourself you want out of life, it may very well be that these 'set-in-the-past restrictions' are getting in your way.</u>

In the late 1980's, I had the privilege of editing and assembling a new audio-cassette series featuring the recorded radio broadcasts and lectures of Dr. Maxwell Maltz, famous in the 1950's for his best-selling book,

'Psycho-Cybernetics', in which he advanced the idea that everything from a person's financial success to the accuracy of his golf swing was controlled by a subconsciously held, very detailed "self-image", largely constructed out of childhood programming and experiences, then reinforced through self-talk.

Dr. Maltz was first pointed in this direction while in practice as a cosmetic surgeon; many patients came believing that getting some physical flaw fixed – a nose bobbed, breasts enlarged – would alter the way they felt about themselves and make them happier but even after surgery that made them beautiful or handsome on the outside, they still thought, talked and acted as if nothing had changed. From this observation, Dr. Maltz made the giant leap – now virtually accepted as universal truth – that a person can practice the perfect golf swing, for example, all he wants and still suffer an awesome slice, unless and until he somehow alters the *image* he has of himself as a golfer.

There is a kind of mental magnetism connected to the self-image. Earl Nightingale put it this way: *we become what we think about most.* Of course, that's not instantly, literally true; if it were, as a teenager I'd have become Playmate Of The Month. But, over time, it is true. People do think themselves sick or old before their time. Or a victim. A perpetual loser.

Certainly, experience alters the self-image. For years, a person considers himself hopelessly clumsy. Then, out of dire necessity, he picks up tools and fixes something and is shocked to discover the awkward lack of coordination of teenage years has been replaced by reasonable facility, and he can drive a nail, and now has to question the long-held, limiting self-image: *hey, wait a minute, maybe I'm not so clumsy after all.*

There's no reason that has to happen only by happy accident. Instead, you can benefit enormously by testing your limits. *"Let's just see if this is still true."* The more of this you do, the more likely you are to uncover abilities you didn't know you had.

In *"The Hobbit"* Bilbo Baggins said, "I don't like adventures. They make one late for dinner." That is the attitude of far too many people. At age 25, David Smith – college drop-out, gambler, playboy, occasional saloonkeeper, began what he has called a 'healing journey' of exploration. By the time he was 35, he had become the first person to swim from Africa to Europe, had kayaked 2,000 miles down the Nile, run a marathon with tribesmen in Kenya, and put himself through a number of other incredible adventures. (You can read about his story in his book *"Healing Journey: The Odyssey Of An Uncommon Athlete"*, published by Sierra Club Books.) David inscribed the book to me, "to a man who knows the art of adventure." Frankly, I wish that was a bit truer than it actually is. But I do stretch. I do test. Constantly. Why not? Fortunately I grew up hearing "how do you know until you try?" You don't.

Take A Closer Look At
The Labels Sewn On You

Labels get sewn on children – then they often stay on them as they become adults, even though they are no longer correct (if they ever were). Consider these labels:

* Such a CLUMSY AND AWKWARD CHILD

* SLOW LEARNER

* BOOKWORM

* SHY WALLFLOWER...THE QUIET TYPE
* DAYDREAMER
* Just not good with _____

  (math; spelling; sports, etc.)

Or consider these: Clint Eastwood was told by an executive at Universal Pictures that he "had no future as an actor" because he had a chipped tooth, an Adams apple that was too prominent, and talked too slow. Best-selling, millionaire author Scott Turow *("Presumed Innocent")* must be a shock to his high school English teacher; Scott got an "F" in that course. In his first fight, Joe Louis was knocked down six times in three rounds, and labeled by one

sportswriter as a "doormat with no future." Charles Schultz, creator of *"Peanuts"*, was turned down for a job as a cartoonist at the Disney Studios, and told he "lacked talent".

What Life's Winners Do About Their Labels: The Artichoke Factor

The labels of football teams are interesting. In many cases, there are images invoked for the players to live up to. The Oakland Raiders, for example, with the pirate logo, silver and black colors, "Raiders" name, all that calls for a very tough, aggressive, physical style of play. Players have talked about there being something "special" about that tradition; they've said that when you put on a Raiders uniform, something happens to you inside. For years, the Pittsburgh Steelers were famous for their "Steel Curtain Defense." For obvious reasons, you'll probably never see a football team named "The Williamsburg Librarians."

Which brings us to the small Scottsdale Community College, in 1975, with a very liberal student body opposed to competitive sports. They considered football frivolous, superficial and representative of a too-violent, too-male-dominated society. As a symbol of their feelings, they elected the artichoke as the official mascot of the college's football team. Imagine the ridicule you'd suffer suiting up and taking the field as a player on The Scottsdale Artichokes!

The Artichokes played their games at a local high school, because their own practice field had no bleachers, and no funds were ever approved for any. Their head coach, John Aviantos, had no scholarships to offer in recruiting talented players. Burdened with the artichoke name, given no recruiting tools, minimal funds, Coach Aviantos still won four conference championships, went to two bowl games, and never had a losing season.

Coach Aviantos coined the term "The Artichoke Factor" to represent the aspect of a person's character that inspires him to rise to a challenge, to look at the labels that have been sewn on, disagree, and tear them off. **"Successful people rarely start out labeled as most-likely-to-succeed,"** Coach told me. In the sixth year of his tenure there, an 8-foot-high sculpture of an artichoke was erected – a monument to Aviantos' determination not to let a negative, humiliating label stay sewn on his football program and his players.

Labels Sewn On "Accidentally" In Childhood Are One Thing – Labels Attached To Us As Adults Are Another

The CBS news anchor Dan Rather once commented that one of the most shocking lessons in life is the discovery that not everyone wishes you well. There is a surprising amount of jealousy, envy and resentment directed at high achievers in every field. The more you try to do and the more you do, the more you will be subject to it.

Consider the "Idiot" label that the media tried so hard to sew onto former Vice-President Dan Quayle. His words and actions were scrutinized with microscopic intensity for the express purpose of "catching" something that could be used to get another stitch sewn with that label. (Years ago, I listened as V.P. Al Gore gave a long, rambling, meaningless, confused answer to a question on *"Meet The Press"* and was not challenged then, nor did anyone comment on it later. Had it been Quayle it would have been front page news.) Quayle defied the label with a mixture of humor, quiet confidence, determination and strategic action, and refused to let it limit or interfere with his actions.

As I mentioned in this book's introduction, the "Washed Up Has-Been" label was sewn on Joan Rivers after the loss of her talk show and the suicide of her husband, and it was sewn on by her own agent and manager, many 'supposed' friends, and the media. Joan defied the label with grit, hard work, a willingness to go through any door of opportunity she could find, humor, talent and self-confidence. She refused to let her actions be limited or dictated by the label others were so eager to attach to her.

In preparation for another book, I did considerable research on Debbi Fields, founder of Mrs. Fields Cookies. She and I also appeared as speakers on several events together. Debbie is arguably one of the best known, most widely recognized, and most phenomenally successful women entrepreneurs of our time. But in the beginning she was labeled as an "empty-headed housewife" by her husband's business acquaintances, bankers, family, "friends", vendors and suppliers.

Fran Tarkenton, who I've gotten to know thanks to a number of Guthy-Renker Corporation projects, was labeled "too small to play in the NFL." Today's quarterbacks are still scrambling to catch up to some of his records. Doug Flutie, a collegiate football superstar, was labeled "too small" to play pro ball by the NFL. He then went on to become THE most valuable player – with his multi-million dollar arm – in the expanding Canadian Football League and eventually on to a successful career in the NFL.

It seems that the world is eager to attach labels; too old….too young…. too small….too big….too slow….too dumb….too clumsy….too inexperienced….too this-or-that. You've just about got to keep one eye open while you sleep because somebody may be sneaking up to try and label you.

It is important to note that successful people tend to defy their labels past and present with their actions. Unsuccessful people accept and conform to their labels, by their actions.

- Dan Kennedy

In the words of Mande White...

Apologies First…

I should start my chapter apologizing for what you are about to read. Writing these few pages feels like torture for me and for 6 weeks I've found all kinds of ways to procrastinate. But the time has come and so, with fingers crossed, I'm hoping that by writing this I'll discover a new capability.

> ### *"Thinking will not overcome fear but action will."*
> W. Clement Stone

Why would I start my chapter this way? Isn't this supposed to be a book on success?

Stay with me here, the moral of this story is quite fitting and I hope, ultimately, to be inspirational...

I wear a lot of labels sewn on me with various words like "BAD WRITER" and "HATES TO WRITE". In the past, I have often times let them incapacitate me and keep me playing small and safe.

Yet, as a follower of Dan Kennedy, I keep putting myself in scenarios (like this) where I MUST do what I don't like to do because I want the outcome (becoming a published author with Dan Kennedy) and I know with time the pain will subside.

That's also why I've committed to writing posts and articles for a number of blogs that I maintain or contribute to. It forces me to take action. The whole time I'm writing, I usually have conversations or arguments with those labels as they fight to stay on and keep me from doing what I know I need to do.

I know these labels were sewn on during childhood as I have some vague memory of someone very important to me telling me I wasn't good at writing...that I shouldn't be writing and they should help me from now on.

For many years, I played victim to that label. I surrounded myself with people who reinforced those labels and they were always eager and willing to help me with the writing (often doing most of it themselves). But with every homework assignment that was turned in, every proposal or report that was not 100% my work….good or bad…I knew I was telling myself every time, that I couldn't do it…that I couldn't figure it out on my own.

From Sitting on the Sidelines to Staring in the Game…The Turning Point

I've been an observer of Dan Kennedy and GKIC since 2006. Mostly just reading the No B.S. Marketing newsletter and then setting them on a shelf, not 'doing' any of that type of marketing for myself or any business I worked with. Not spending any time with other GKIC members to fan the flame of desire and accomplishment. But in late 2008, I found myself in South Florida with every opportunity to start my professional life over…

Rewind to 2004…I had moved to South Florida to take a job as a Marketing Director for a Pilates Teacher Training program and for various reasons didn't stay there long but during that time I had gotten involved with the local American Marketing Association of South Florida and was even elected onto the Board of Directors.

At the time, I was looking for a new job and really wanting to spread my horizons from not only marketing products and services that I loved, but to really understanding what makes people buy what they do. Plus, I wanted to find a way to implement all the GKIC-style marketing that I had read about. Luckily and unknowingly, I found myself in the "SPAM Capital of the World". (For those of you who are unfamiliar with SPAM, I'm not referring to the canned meat product, I'm referring to unsolicited email marketing.) So I took a job at an Internet Marketing company and was immediately thrown into the bowels of the industry.

I remember going home the first night and crying because I really didn't believe in what advertisements and offers I was brokering. I thought...*I wouldn't waste my money on this...why should anyone else?*

The Unexpected Secret to Success Revealed

Then one day when I came into work and saw that over $100,000 of traffic had been driven to my advertisements and over 15,000 leads, I decided to stop being judgmental. Something about this scenario worked and I was limiting myself if I chose not to be a part of it and limit myself by 'what I would or would not do'.

For the next few years, my job was to match Internet traffic sources with advertisements and offers. I quickly had to learn what sources of traffic were good for which types of advertisements and what elements made an advertisement or offer successful. As long as I removed my judgment from the situation and relied about the theory of 'getting into the prospects head' I matched successful advertisement to successful traffic source!

It was amazing that Internet marketing is not only an art but also a science. To truly master the media, you must not only understand marketing but, psychology and technology as well. Because of this and my very analytic MBA mind, I found it best to let others be good at what they were good at, liking driving traffic, as I wanted to focus on building offers to match and fit the traffic they were so good at driving.

I did exactly this at an offline list brokerage company for the next few years. There I worked with traditional direct mailers and helped them transition their successful offline offers to successful online offers. It was an exciting adventure as I built my own Co-Registration path and Cost Per Lead and

Cost Per Acquisition lead generation offers. I even directed the team that set up an email marketing division for the list management company.

During this adventure of building offers, I dove fully back into GKIC-style marketing and decided to join the local Renegade South Florida Entrepreneur / GKIC Miami Chapter for additional support. It was there I found my home...a place where test, tracking and tweaking outrageous offers, compelling headlines and media is not at all out of the ordinary. In fact, you were abnormal if you weren't constantly stepping up your game. With Andrew Cass as Chapter Director, the meetings are packed with brilliant content.

Being part of the local Miami Chapter gave me the opportunity to attend the Phenomenon event in Orlando in January 2009. This was pivotal for me for several reasons.

First, I saw 12 examples of people who had stepped forward and took action, often imperfect action, and achieved more in 12 months than in the previous 12 years. Each person, verifying that by not allowing the fear to incapacitate them and taking action, massive action, their future was dramatically altered.

Second, I really got to know my local Renegade South Florida Entrepreneur / GKIC Miami Chapter Members and found a group of people that were doing the same things I was doing. They 'got' me and I them. They 'got' that being a solo entrepreneur is a journey and one that can take the form of as much self-reflection as desired. They 'got' that breakdowns come before the breakthroughs.

I 'got' that the labels sewn on me they didn't see. Now this one took awhile and often still does and you can still find me going around showing my "SUCKS at WRITING" label to others (Am I doing that here?) and getting a response back like "What are you crazy?!"

Third, our Chapter Director, Andrew Cass, communicated that "action not excuses" is where we got the results. He never responded to my self-proclaimed labels. He encouraged me to practice and implement then practice and implement some more. He acknowledged my growth, as my writing got better. He made the space for there to be another label, a more empowering label to be acknowledged. Maybe that'll be "Profitable Writer!"

Discovering MY Super Power...

Have you heard the Louis Armstrong song, "Let's Call the Whole Thing Off" where two people are arguing or how a word is pronounced?

You like potato *and I like potahto, You like tomato and I like tomahto*

Well, I've found that it's not so much the way you SAY something that gives it power, but in <u>what you make it mean.</u>

We as humans created language to communicate but it's really only in the language that meaning is given. And the meaning is really what gives power to a word/label or not.

Ever hear of Dr. Masaru Emoto and his book *The Message from Water?* In his experiments he took water and studied the way the cells looked after labeling the containers of water. Some he labeled with negative worlds like curse words and others he labeled with positive words like "love" "joy" and "happiness". After just a short period of time the cells of the water changed the way they looked. The water labeled with the curse words took an ugly shape and the water labeled with positive words took on a beautiful shape, much like a snowflake.

Since our body is mostly made of water…and there are emotion molecules in every cell of our body (check out *Molecules of Emotion* by Candace Pert for a fascinating read), doesn't it make sense that our greatest super powers as human beings right now is the <u>attention</u> we give to our thoughts?

Now, someone can tell me I'm a bad writer and for a second it might sting but quickly I can move to a place of knowing that my writing has filled numerous workshops and tele-seminars. I have sold a respectable number of information products with my writing and it has inspired and encouraged hundreds if not thousands of people to go out and do something that scares them or that they thought wasn't possible.

This brings me to one of my favorite quotes from Dan Kennedy that really shifted my mindset and my income.

"Only take advice from those people who are paying you money OR are making more money than you."

The others are just jealous. Only you have the ability to give your labels power.

Trying On New Labels

As a kid, I moved around a lot. Every time my mother told me that whenever I started school in a new place, the first day I walked into school I could "BE" whoever I wanted to be. If in the last school I had been shy and isolated then in this new school I could be outgoing and friendly.

In order to 'be' outgoing and friendly I had to DO different things than I had in the last place. I had to go up to people and say hello. I had to ask them questions and find something to talk about with them. As I found what actions worked for me. I found myself having the relationships and experiences that I wanted. I was then labeled as "friendly" and "outgoing".

I teach this same exercise to my clients when they are networking online or offline. How can you sew different labels on yourself? Let me give you another personal example, we'll use my previous "BAD writer" label...

First you BE. This isn't just a positive affirmation. It's more of recognizing that you really are anything you want to be once you remove the labels from childhood that are taking up space for you to just be anything you want to be.

So for me, I create the space that "I am a GOOD writer! I LIKE to write! It's important for me to write, even if it isn't perfect because people want to hear what I have to say."

Notice this is more than a positive affirmation. I'm not saying anything I'm not in agreement with. I'm not congruent with "loving" writing yet...that'll come later, and its ok to just like it for now. 'Liking it' still gets the bills paid. Loving it will probably help create its own 6 or 7 figure income stream though!

Next, I DO the things that writers I like and admire do, like practice writing daily, voraciously reading. Sometimes I re-write the things they have written to get my subconscious to pay attention. Next, I actively search for people that want to hear what I have to say and ignore those that don't. Lastly, I press "send" or "publish" on that email or blog post so that the content is live for the world to see and not just safely saved on my hard drive.

After 2 years of blogging for FreeSocialMediaHelp.com and NoBSMiami.com/blog, I have a group of loyal followers who know, like and trust me to provide them with honest advice and helpful tips. I have gotten to the place where I'm able to send an email and generate money on demand and even make money while I'm on vacation. It's a process and journey but the self-development and adventure are sure worth it.

Bottom Line...

What labels will you take immediate and decisive action on dissolving or disempowering? What labels can you proudly sew on yourself so that you can step into being all that you really are?

- Mande White

Mande created her first information product in 2001 and has since spent the last 10 years behind the scenes of some of the most successful Internet Marketers advising on strategy, product offerings, traffic methods and conversion techniques.

Mande has helped generate over 10,000,000 leads resulting in over $20 million is additional revenue for her clients since 2001.

She makes money 24/7/365 from the information products she has created in her "Magic Bullet" series including: LinkedIn Magic Bullet, Income Magic Bullet, Facebook Magic Bullet, and over a dozen more! You can find out about all her products and programs at www.MandeWhite.com. You can request a FREE copy of her Marketing Magic Bullet program (a $297 value) by visiting: www.FreeGiftFromMande.com/UltimateSuccess

---

"Sadly, most people are unconscious to the labels they've had put upon them and stay stuck never reaching their full potential."

- Andrew J. Cass

"Want to know where to find your next big opportunity? It's waiting for you out there just beyond the boundaries of your current comfort zone."

- RJon Robins

"Not all labels are negative. Some labels are earned through what you excel at. The challenge comes when you choose to change your focus and direction to something *new*, where you're not recognized and have no track record yet."

- Carlos Castellanos

"The hardest label I've had to fight is that of being 'too smart for my own good'. When I find myself suffering from analysis paralysis, taking ANY sort of action is the only remedy."

- Mande White

"Believe that all things work together for your good and it will open the door to a realm of possibilities."

- Christine Myers

"It's unfortunate that we can self-sabotage using mis-information that we picked up during our childhood. In way too many spheres of human endeavor there's too much emphasis on the physical cultivation to the detriment of the need for high levels of mental cultivation."

- Dwight Woods

"What is the anchor, baggage, label, or self-imposed CHOKE HOLD that is preventing you from achieving your greatness? Take the time and figure out what it is for you and conquer it."

- Debbie Wysocki

"We surely are what we think we are."

- John Tate

"Lao Tzu said: '*The journey of a thousand miles must begin with a single step.*' And the only one to make that step is you."

- Alle van Calker

CHAPTER 6

TAKE ACTION TO GET PAID

By Dan Kennedy

O ne of the most interesting metaphysical authors, Stuart Wilde, says, "When they show up, *bill 'em.*" What does that mean? It actually refers as much to overriding attitude as to business policy.

One meaning is to properly value your time. If you do not place a high value on your time, I can promise you no one else will either. Yet, the one thing we all have an equal amount of is time. Everybody starts out each day with 24 hours to invest as wisely as possible, for profit, for joy, for the benefit of others. The richest man in the world gets not a minute more to work with than does

the poorest beggar on the street. But you can bet everything you've got that he thinks about that time differently, feels about that time differently, allocates that time differently, and has an entirely different intellectual, emotional, physical and actual experience with time than does the beggar. There's the rub; to get from poor to rich, you have to adopt the attitudes about time of the rich.

Another meaning, a bigger one, is to value yourself.

When I first started in the 'success education business', one of the few people in the country who was consistently effective at selling self-improvement audio cassette programs direct, face to face, to executives and sales-people gave me what turned out to be very, very good advice – he said: "Don't waste your time trying to sell these materials to the people who need it most. They won't buy it. You should focus on selling to successful people who want to get even better."

Over the years, I've demonstrated the validity of this to myself a number of different ways. And I've developed an explanation for it. There is what I now call "the self-esteem Catch-22 loop" at work here: in order for a person to invest directly in himself, which is what buying self-improvement materials is, he has to place value on himself, i.e. have high self-esteem, but if he has such high self-esteem, he is probably already doing well and does not have a critical need for this type of information; he will get marginal improvement out of it; but the person who needs it most does not place much value on himself, i.e. has relatively low self-esteem which prohibits him from buying, believing in or using self-improvement materials.

At a very practical level, I see this "value hang-up" surface all the time with entrepreneurs, authors, speakers, consultants, doctors dealing with fees and prices. I understand it. I still remember the first time I quoted a client $15,000 to develop a direct-mail campaign for him, held my breath, and instantly thought to myself *"Geez, Kennedy, a lot of people work all year to make that much money. What business do YOU have asking for that for a few days' work? Who do you think you are anyway?"* But here's the amazing thing: the world largely accepts YOUR appraisal of your value, and just about everybody under-values and under-prices their contributions.

My good friend Rodney Tolleson was very active for a handful of years in the practice management business, providing doctors of chiropractic with a comprehensive collection of business-building services, training and counseling. I worked with him doing many of the seminars. We both discovered that these "professionals" were no different than anyone else; they had incredible mental and emotional blocks about charging what they and their service were worth. Although his company provided them with enormously helpful technical, management and marketing assistance and tools, the greatest income leaps were achieved by focusing on the doctors' beliefs about worth and value – "practice esteem" and "self esteem." There was more 'fee resistance' in the doctors' minds than in the publics. And all their actions relative to promoting the practice, stimulating referrals, setting, asking for and promptly collecting fees, insisting on compliance with recommendations were governed – hindered – by their surprisingly low self-appraisals.

A 'No B.S. Marketing Letter' Subscriber & GKIC Member Hits The Nail On The Head...

I'm fortunate to have tens of thousands of GKIC Members and Subscribers who are bright, curious, innovative, and contributive, so ours is more of a continuing dialogue than just my publishing a newsletter. One such Member is David Garfinkel, the President of a consulting firm named 'Let Your Clients Do Your Selling.' When I got into the final stages of this book, I invited my Members to submit their ideas about "the ultimate secret of success." David's suggestion was most interesting. And, while it does not name "the ultimate secret", it does hit the nail on the head about the chief obstacle to benefiting from that secret.

David said, "After all the smoke clears, it gets down to one thing – one limiting belief – one self-concept that, once revamped, will set you off on a permanent success trajectory, I think that's different for each of us, but it's usually a personal version of the feeling 'Yes, I really CAN succeed.' "

I agree. For more than 15 years, I have explained that we live inside two boxes:

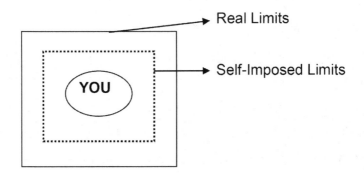

The solid, outer boundary represents **REAL LIMITS,** and we all have some real limits. At the time of this book's original publishing, the oldest active player in the NFL is Brett Favre, a quarterback for the Minnesota Vikings – Brett is 41 years old. Still, I really CAN'T go try out and make the roster of an NFL team. Even if I trained for the next 12 months, I still couldn't do it. Brett has stayed in peak condition and played his entire life. I didn't play in high school (I didn't go to college), I rarely exercise and haven't "worked out" in years, I have chronic back problems, one bad knee, and well, I'd go out of the tryout on a stretcher. I just cannot play pro football, no matter how much I may "desire" it – unless I buy a team. Even then, I probably wouldn't get through a series of downs. That IS a REAL limit.

As of now, you CAN'T do business on Mars. That's a REAL limit.

But way inside that solid line, real boundary is the dotted line. The dotted line represents the **SELF-IMPOSED LIMITS.** This is a much smaller box we build around ourselves. It's made up of "IF", "CAN'T, "IMPOSSIBLE" inaccurately applied, of negatives in "The Big 4 Of Life": Self-Esteem, Self-Image, Self-Confidence and Self-Discipline. But David's suggestion adds a new wrinkle to all this; that there is ONE "dot" on this dotted line that is bolder, blacker, bigger and more significant than all the others... and that when you bust through it, the entire dotted line box disappears.

In monetary terms, that dotted line certainly controls how much value you place on yourself, your time, your know-how and your services, how much you dare demand, and how much you get. Anytime you push that box out, you automatically increase your income. Now I would suggest that the biggest leap can come from pushing against it at the point where it seems strongest.

"Abundance" Doesn't Care

Liberals constantly try to demonize exceptional ambition and achievement. This follows a liberal theme that the economy is and must be "win-lose" and if one person gets "too rich" that must somehow force others to become poor or poorer. This kind of class divisiveness may be necessary politics for the liberals, but it is economic nonsense. And, unfortunately, this is one of the ways people build up guilt about striving for and achieving extraordinary successes.

Foster Hibbard often talks about two men going down to the ocean, one with a teaspoon, the other with a bucket, each taking away the amount of water he chooses to take away. The ocean, however, doesn't care. The ocean doesn't care if you come down there with a teaspoon, bucket or tanker truck. The ocean is a miraculously replenishing, unlimited resource. That represents ABUNDANCE. And Abundance doesn't care either. It matters not to Abundance whether you tap into it a little or a lot. Your "withdrawals" don't diminish anyone else's opportunities nor do they damage the total amount of available abundance. It is infinite. Infinite! And the only limits on "your share" are placed on you by you.

- Dan Kennedy

"So many people place so little value on themselves nowadays it's frightening."

- Andrew J. Cass

"Placing a high value on your time, or your product or your seminar or your service or whatever it is you do has the beneficial effect of forcing your internal integrity to find a ways to live-up to that value. Pricing yourself too cheaply tends to have the exact opposite effect and is a disservice to your customers and clients who need you to be at your best."

- RJon Robins

"Many artists undercharge because what they do comes so easy to them. The truth is, that which comes easiest to you should be what you charge most for."

- Carlos Castellanos

"For me, this journey is like a roller coaster. Every time I raise my prices or step into something bigger, the anticipation is so SCARY until the moment that someone accepts that new price or opportunity. Then the exhilaration of the new possibility removes all memory of the previous fear….until the next time."

- Mande White

"A favorite quote of mine: 'Nothing is a waste of time if you use the experience wisely' by Rodin"

- Christine Myers

"In my field, martial arts, it took me a while to realize that training the art of SELF-defense can lead to improvements in SELF-esteem, SELF-image, SELF-discipline and most any other desirable quality prefixed with the word SELF."

- Dwight Woods

"How many times do you let the 'Big 3' (IF, CAN'T, and IMPOSSIBLE… combine with Self-Esteem, Self-Image, Self-Confidence, and Self-Discipline)? It's our limiting beliefs that hold us back. Henry Ford says 'Think you can; think you can't; either way you're right.' What limit have you placed on yourself?"

- Debbie Wysocki

"I was fortunate enough to have a life altering near death experience. While lying in the hospital bed, a question occurred to me that I still ask myself to this day. The question is, 'Why not me?' Meaning, why shouldn't I achieve something or have something that I might have previously thought only suited for 'other people'."

- John Tate

"He who complains loses his opportunity."

- Alle van Calker

WHAT YOU ARE WILLING TO ACCEPT IS WHAT YOU GET.

CHAPTER 7

TAKE ACTION TO WIN OVER WORRY

By Dan Kennedy and Alle van Calker

I have had a great many misfortunes in my life – but only about half as many as I have painfully anticipated.

Worry can create physical illnesses, stress and fatigue. Worry robs you of your competence and confidence. Many people are literally immobilized by worry.

Yet, as destructive as we know worry to be, and as unnecessary as worrying often proves to be, most people still let worry into their lives virtually every day. Ironically, we give our worries power by thinking about them. The more you worry about something, the more power worry itself gains over you. Even small worries can amass enormous power if you let them. Dr. Edward Kramer observed: **"A penny held to the eye blocks the sun."**

So, how do you eliminate worry from your life?

I'm not sure you can eliminate it. Worry is often the starting point of constructive, creative thought. But you can reduce its time consumption and influence in your life.

You can temporarily do it with chemicals. Booze. Prescription, over-the-counter or street drugs. Personally, I used the drink-to-coma method myself for several years. The problem with that is, when you return to the real world, the things you were worrying about are there waiting for you, and you're further handicapped in dealing with them by the hangovers and other physical debilitation.

This kind of escape yields no real benefit and has its own added costs. I can't speak to the drug thing, as I've never tried any street drugs and very rarely even swallow a Tylenol. But I can talk about alcohol from experience, and I'll only briefly say this: if you find yourself knocking back a few every day, everything you tell yourself about not having a problem is crap. You've got a problem. NOT a solution; a problem. If you protect it and continue with it, it will eventually destroy your business or career, an important relationship, your health or land yourself in jail. If you cannot quickly kick this habit alone, get help.

THE only real antidote for worry is action.

Decision is the empowering opposite of worry. When you take action to solve a problem, you take power away from the problem, and you gain power. For every source of worry and anxiety, there is usually a list of a number of potentially helpful actions. If you'll get involved in making that list and acting on all the items on the list, worry will be eliminated; it cannot co-exist with such constructive action.

I recently read an article about a CEO of a huge company, on the brink of financial ruin, presented with the fact that they had only enough cash to operate the business for another three days. "What then," he asked, "are we going to spend it on?" He was instantly moving on to actions, not worry.

If you find yourself too frequently immobilized by worry, I have a book to recommend: W. Clement Stone's *THE SUCCESS SYSTEM THAT NEVER FAILS*. Pay particular attention to his discussion of the sudden termination of his right to represent a particular company; the end of a business he had struggled mightily to build; an eminent and apparently unmanageable threat to everything he had and everything he had worked for; and how he reacted to it.

But – what about the problem you cannot take any action to resolve? First of all, there's rarely any situation that defies all action. But, for the sake of conversation, let's assume that you are up against something so tough that, at least at the moment, there is absolutely nothing you can do, no action you can take. If that is the case, then the only thing you can do is set that problem aside entirely and take action on some other matter or project that you can do something about.

The ONLY antidote for worry is action.

What about worrying about what others think? A great deal of unhappiness comes from people pursuing and achieving others' goals instead of their own. When I was a kid, one of our neighbors, Ralph F., created a great deal of unhappiness for himself, his wife and his five sons by obsessing over his sons' disinterest in taking over the family business. I wonder how many kids buckle under to such pressure and achieve the goals their parents' set for them – and wind up wishing they hadn't. Working to achieve others' goals set for you, to meet others' expectations, to satisfy others' definitions, which is what you do when you worry about what others think.

My friend Herb True had moved from the academic world to a very successful career in professional speaking, and could have continued to enjoy a growing, exceptional income, create and market CD's, author best-selling books and accumulate wealth. He chose not to. Herb chose to cut his business back to taking just a few speaking engagements a year so he could return to teaching at Notre Dame. When he did so, I know that many of his peers and friends thought he'd lost his marbles. Or gotten too old to compete. Or had the business pass him by. None of those things are true. But regardless of what anybody else or everybody else thought, Herb chose to pursue *his* goals. The result is one of the most contented but invigorated, happy and fulfilled individuals I know or have ever observed.

Oh, and you'd probably be surprised (disappointed?) if you knew how little others think about you. Most people have their hands full dealing with their own lives. They ponder yours a lot less than you probably assume. But regardless of how little or great the world's interest is in how you choose to live your life, "sooner or later you stand in your own space." The cure for worry over others' opinions is taking action that satisfies you and, as a result, increases your sense of control, feeling of power, self-confidence and self-esteem. Others can never gift you with self-esteem or peace of mind. These are products of your own actions.

- Dan Kennedy

In the words of Alle van Calker...

I totally agree what Dan Kennedy explains in this chapter. When I was in my early twenties, worry was a daily "exercise" and did not help me whatsoever.

After finding out that worry really does not change anything, nor will it help you to make decisions, things started to change for me. Not that this worrying disappeared overnight, that took a couple of years. It needs training and experience.

How did I overcome the worry habit? I read a lot of books, for example, from Anthony Robbins to Dr. Wayne Dyer to name a few. This proved to me that different thinking can lead to a different outcome.

I grew up in The Netherlands, which has, as I see it now, a worry culture. I always wanted to start my own business, however, as Dan explained above, others always interfered, said it was a bad idea - what if... what if... what if... - So that was not very helpful.

When I moved to the US, the mentality was totally different. People that you would ask or consult about having your own business where totally supportive. Wow, what a change that was! No one was saying, "but what if?" or, "are you sure you want to do this?"

I think it was about a year and a half after I settled in California that I started my first import-export business. Having a large international network of good friends and business relationships that I built during my job as an export manager for the company I worked for in Holland, gave me the opportunity to serve as a key contact in the US for them. I sourced products from the US and exported them to different countries across the globe.

In the meantime, I was also employed with a company in Santa Barbara CA where I sold environmental research equipment, made by my previous Dutch employer. After a couple of years working in California, I built the US market and really grew their sales. I started to think, "I can do this for myself. I have the experience, the knowledge of the products." The decision was made. I quit my job and continued full time with my own business. Still selling the environmental research equipment from Eijkelkamp in the Netherlands and still importing and exporting all kind of research- and scientific products.

Did I worry during the past few years about having my own business and depending on my clients to earn a living? Sure did, but when I don't like something, I now take massive action and make the change to something I like or can agree with. It does not have to be perfect right away, but taking action and making a change, is a good way to start.

For example, now having my own business selling environmental research equipment, I needed to expand my customer base. I had a website but that was it and I did not do enough marketing. At that time I had become a member of GKIC and the Renegade South Florida Entrepreneurs / GKIC Miami Chapter, as well as one of Andrew Cass's private Mastermind Group Members. I learned so much, took action, and implemented. I saw my revenue double in one year.

Now I get start to *"worry"* about how to handle how fast my business is growing!

Alle van Calker is the owner and president of Sunvalley Solutions Inc. Sampling Solutions Made Easy, 'By Digging a Little Deeper for You.'

Representing the world famous Eijkelkamp Agrisearch Equipment BV from the Netherlands, SDEC from France and Umwelt Geraete Technik from Germany, we make a complete line of high quality products available for research in Soil, Water and Groundwater.

For more information visit: www.sunvalleysolutions.com or call 305-677-3325

"I think people spend more time *worrying* about what may never be than they do *planning* what could be. I find that to be backwards."

- Andrew J. Cass

"A minute spent thinking about someone else's business comes at the cost of an hour that could be invested thinking about your own."

- RJon Robins

"The biggest energy dump is worrying over those things you are not willing to change or take action on."

- Carlos Castellanos

"Hopefully the point of this chapter is clear. The only real antidote for worry is action. So go do something already!"

- Mande White

"Replace worry by thinking about the desired results. Start working on the solution rather than a possible negative outcome.

- Christine Myers

"I believe in 'constructive worrying.' Going over the possible 'what if?' scenarios can sometimes lead to a hitherto unrecognized solution to your problem."

- Dwight Woods

"Worry wastes time – and can make you sick. Nonetheless, it's a real emotion that afflicts nearly everyone – to what degree is up to you. For some it's crippling. The ONLY cure for worry is action. When you identify the challenge, identify possible solutions, and take the action to implement them NOW. You will quickly go from WORST CASE (and worry) to BETTER scenario."

- Debbie Wysocki

"It is funny the power of simply making a list. Whether it is a list of tasks toward overcoming a worry, or a list of your top six tasks for the day ahead, the list makes it seem much less daunting."

- John Tate

"When the time comes, it will be OK"

- Alle van Calker

CHAPTER 8

A COMMONALITY AMONG THOSE WHO STRUGGLE THE MOST

By Andrew J. Cass

I teach, train, and speak nationally on Direct Response Marketing and Direct Sales. At the time of this writing, I'm entering my 17th year in the business of 'commission-only' Direct Sales. In all that time, I have not ever been given a company paycheck (w-2) and I've supported myself selling for almost <u>two decades</u>. Twice in that time frame, in two separate fields, I cracked the 7-figure mark, before the age of 35. Very few can say the same...

[I launched and now publish the first-ever iPad Magazine on the topic of "selling" in the New Economy, *Direct Selling Insider,*™ now featured on the Apple Newsstand. For more information and to get a complimentary issue visit: <u>www.DirectSellingInsider.com</u>]

...I tell you this because in all of the sales and marketing training I do with Entrepreneurs, I see <u>one</u> common pattern in those who struggle the most, one commonality: they "procrastinate" the most. They take the *least* amount of action, but have the *most* excuses and stories as to why they aren't getting ahead.

As Dan Kennedy and a few of our co-authors have pointed out in the last few chapters, it's actually more action, more activity, and more movement that *eliminates* struggle. And worry. And fear. It's not less action. Yet, those struggling the most tend to actually do the least...

Often times, it's a direct result of NOT being real *clear* on where they are going and NOT having a system or a game plan to get there. They're usually scattered, running in a million different directions, always in "reaction mode." I'm sure you've felt this way before. We all have. And do. And in the Information Age, with all we have coming at us a mile-a minute, *that* feeling isn't going away any time soon. We need to embrace it and manage it. Most get upset by it and freeze up.

The key is to be in motion, movin' and shakin' as often as possible. Moving faster, not slower. Getting out of your comfort zone. Exploring new ways of doing things. Being open to new ideas... so you don't get *stuck*, which leads to overwhelm, which then leads to procrastination – a vicious downward spiral...

In addition to high-quality sales and marketing content, I routinely bring the very best training and solutions on **clarity** and **focus** in business to my local Renegade South Florida Entrepreneurs / GKIC Miami Chapter members and private mastermind members on a monthly basis at our live events here in South Florida (more information can be found at: www.NoBSMiami.com).

There is NOT a more important topic nowadays as we move deeper and deeper into the Information Age and will, undoubtedly, have more and more distractions coming at us. It's how we deal with distractions and persevere in the face of adversity that will dictate how successful we *can* become.

- Andrew J. Cass

Come dear, he may be contagious.

CHAPTER 9

TAKE ACTION WHEN YOUR INNER VOICE SPEAKS

By Dan Kennedy and Dwight Woods

About 40 years ago, an expectant mother took a $500.00 risk and placed a little ad in *"Seventeen Magazine"'* for a new purse monogrammed with the customer's initials. She believed in her idea and acted on it, even though $500.00 was a great deal of money for her at the time, even though she had no market research to support it, even though she had no business experience. Her little ad produced $32,000.00 in orders. And these days her Lillian Vernon Company sells more than $150 million dollars of merchandise each year.

In a speech to the New York Venture group on May 17, 1990, Lillian Vernon said, "I make quick decisions. I take chances, relying on what I consider my *golden gut*."

She went on to say: "Growing from a million dollar to a multi-million dollar company involved areas such as finance, list management, computers and large-scale production realms beyond my expertise. I tried to cover my shortcomings by surrounding myself with experienced veterans of large corporate cultures, usually from outside the direct marketing industry. There were so few direct marketers in the early 1970's that I filled my ranks with managers from different walks of life who generally were very savvy to the ways of big business --- and most of them almost

killed us. I don't want to generalize but some of the corporate executives I hired just couldn't make a decision. They took analysis to the point of paralysis. Every consideration had to first be studied by a committee. In my business, sending a good idea to a committee is like sending Rip Van Winkle to a slumber party. I hate more than anything to wake up and find that one of my competitors is already doing something I was planning on." Lillian Vernon continues to pick winning products for her catalogs today, often trusting her 'golden gut' and making fast decisions.

Confident decisiveness is one of the most prized qualities in the business world. All great leaders exhibit it. People naturally respond to such a person. It is easy for the decisive individual to inspire trust and cooperation. Where does this kind of confident decisiveness come from? Call it what you will: intuition, the golden gut, the inner voice, insight – most exceptionally successful people admit to listening to a secret, inner advisor.

A Few Thoughts About "Insight"*

"The mind can only proceed so far upon what it knows, and can prove. There comes a point where the mind takes a leap --- call it intuition or what you will --- and comes out on a higher plane of knowledge."

– Albert Einstein

My friend and speaking colleague Lee Milteer wrote an outstanding book, *Success Is An Inside Job*, and I thought excerpts from its chapter on *"Intuition: Your Secret Talent"* would be appropriate here:

"It is interesting that in our western culture we seem to comprehend almost all of our experiences through the logical, linear,

analytical thinking process. We use words to communicate this kind of thinking. Because words are our way of understanding our world, we've almost forgotten we have an intuitive, creative part of ourselves. We're not trained to say I FEEL but rather I THINK. If we deny and cut off our intuition, then we get trapped by concepts learned through our programmed minds. Yesterday's learned beliefs (alone) cannot solve today's challenges or enable us to capitalize on tomorrow's opportunities.

Today more and more successful people --- executives, artists, and entrepreneurs, are realizing that making decisions is not an exclusive function of the analytical left side of the brain. You must now use the intuitive and creative right side of your brain as well. You must have an integration of analytical and intuitive thinking. This is commonly referred to as 'whole brain thinking.' Dr. Jonas Salk said, 'A new way of thinking is now needed to deal with our present reality. Our subjective responses (intuitive) are more sensitive and more rapid than our objective responses (reasoned). This is the nature of the way the mind works. We first sense, then we reason why.

I suggest that you have some fun in your life and start testing your intuitive abilities. When the phone rings, ask yourself who it is before you answer – see how many times you're right. When waiting for an elevator, guess which one will come

first. There are dozens of small games you can play with yourself to strengthen your abilities. Your 'intuitive muscle' gets stronger as you use it. Then, when you need your intuition, you will feel more confident in using it.

In his book 'The Intuitive Edge', Philip Goldberg noted '...astonishing speed with which the truly intuitive mind can bring together bits of information only remotely related in time and meaning to form the sudden hunch or whispered feeling that we call intuition.' Conrad Hilton, who was well known for using his intuition in his hotel business, wrote 'I know when I have a problem and have done all I can to figure it out, I keep listening in a sort of inside silence till something clicks and I feel a right answer.' "

Here are some of Lee's Action tips for Encouraging your intuition:

- Listen to your body; that's why we call intuition a 'gut' feeling. The solar plexus is a large network of nerves located behind the stomach and is said to be the seat of emotion. You can have an accurate, gut-level reaction to many situations.
- Allow yourself to re-define the problem frequently; writing out the problem gives you the opportunity to see the
- problem from a different perspective.
- Allow yourself to play. You don't have to be sitting in your office to come up with creative and intuitive solutions. Take a walk, feed the

birds, play hooky for an hour and then come back to work on the problem.

• Take action on your insights. Start investigating with the approach of "will this hunch logically work?"

Two of the self-help pioneers that I've long been a serious student of, Napoleon Hill and Dr. Edward Kramer, both promote reliance on insight and intuition. I don't often talk about it, but I often act on little "flashes" that come to me seemingly out of the blue. I'll give you an example:

Earlier this year, at the second "Jeff Paul Tells All" Mail-Order Seminar we sponsored, one of the attendees was a long-time subscriber and 'student' of mine, Dr. Michael Anderson, owner of a very successful chiropractic practice management company. During the two days of the seminar, I heard about his goals and objectives. On my flight home, a "flash" came – I'll bet Dr. Anderson would buy my SuccessTrak business, notably including my *Practice Building Secrets Newsletter* for chiropractors. Prior to that "flash", I had not even thought out spinning that business off, although I was gradually recognizing that it was no longer a good fit with my other interests and activities and was, therefore, being neglected. As I thought about this "flash", I developed an argument in my mind for synergy between Dr. Anderson's current business and goals and what I had to offer, that made mine worth more to him than it was to me. Most importantly, immediately on my arrival at home, I generated a letter to Dr. Anderson suggesting the deal. And a win-win deal was consummated in a matter of weeks.

For me, this is not at all unusual. These "flashes" frequently occur, I frequently act on them quickly, and I frequently benefit as a result. Consequently, I'm a believer in the role of "intuition" in otherwise hard-nosed, tough-minded, pragmatic business environments. And I find information on the subject, such as that Lee has assembled in her book, of great value.

(You can find information about Lee's books at www.LeeMilteer.com)

How To Use The Miraculous "Dominant Thought Principle" To Energize Your Inner Advisor

I will try to tell this true-life story as briefly as possible: in my hometown of Akron, Ohio, a prominent judge, respected citizen, family man, wound up on the front page of *The Akron Beacon Journal* and in prison, as a child molester. This was 20 years ago; we were still shocked by such things. He was asked how a man like him could wind up in such a horrible situation. He described a "process" --- he said, "One day, years ago, I was out watering my lawn, a little girl in a sundress went by and for a fleeting millisecond I thought about what it would be like with her --- then, of course, I pushed it from my mind. But a year or so later, at a mall, another little girl, and I held the thought for maybe a minute." He went on to mention another incident, a few minutes of thought. Another incident, 15 or 20 minutes of thought. "Then one day," he said, "I woke up and found it was all I was thinking about. For days, it dominated my thoughts. Then I did it."

This is a NEGATIVE example of the amazing power of Dominant Thought.

After 20 years of intense research into what made super successful people tick, Napoleon Hill wrote: "Our brains become magnetized with the dominating thoughts which we hold in our minds, and by means which no man is familiar, these magnets attract to us the forces, the people, the circumstances of life which harmonize with the nature of our dominating thoughts."

I know this to be true, personally, in its positive and its negative application. When you come to grips with this Dominant Thought Principle, you have the "supercharger device" for dramatically accelerating the achievement of any objective; instead of taking weeks, months or years to move from first, fleeting thought to dominant thought, deliberately utilize dominant thought --- because the lapse of time between dominant thought, action and achievement is minimal. All the time is taken up in getting to dominant thought. Very little time is required to get from dominant thought to reality.

Beyond this, dominant thoughts energize your Inner Advisor. Your dominant thoughts are your Inner Advisor's directives. Your dominant thoughts tell your Inner Advisor what to work on. Your Inner Advisor then jumps into action; mobilizes all the vast resources of your subconscious mind, your memory, your experience, your connection to universal intelligence. Then your Inner Advisor tells you precisely what to do, who to call, where to go and when to act, to get from dominant thought to reality as rapidly as possible. When you energize your Inner Advisor with deliberate dominant thought, you can trust and confidently, decisively, <u>act on</u> the Advisor's recommendations.

- Dan Kennedy

_____

In the words of Dwight Woods...

In my industry, the world of martial arts, the desire to learn how to protect themselves and/or their loved ones, leads many people to begin the study and practice of the art of self-defense.

When I conduct my initial interview with a new, prospective student, the topic of intuition invariably comes up. Why? Because in introducing our Academy to new students, we always invite them to pay a visit to meet with the Head Instructor, to take a tour of the school and have an opportunity to get an answer to all of the questions they may have about getting started in martial arts.

We do this because we want to train them, from the very beginning, to always trust their intuition. In a very literal sense, when it comes to self-defense, the use of intuition can be a lifesaver.

Let's say you go somewhere and even though you can't readily identify it, you just "know" something isn't right. Or you meet someone and get the feeling again, that something just isn't right.

You'd be well advised to pay attention to those feelings, to that gut instinct, right? Well, that's the essence of self-defense. Self-defense is a state of mind.

So when someone's interested in joining our Academy, we tell them to come visit us and check us out to see if everything "feels" right. From the very onset, we begin "teaching" self-defense even before someone officially becomes a new member of our Academy. That way, they'll know whether or not we are the right martial art school for them.

The Greatest Computer

As the world becomes more and more technologically advanced, human beings lose more and more of their natural instincts. Even

though many of our greatest minds agree that Man will never be able to create any machine that can equal the computing power of the human brain, we sometimes act as if we need a greater force than our own inner knowledge, to help us in our decision making processes.

In my experience, just about every time we're faced in a situation with a question, we almost always know exactly what we should do in response. Learning to get in tune, to get in sync with our own inner voice is a major step in the direction of greater productivity, achievement and success.

How Formal Education Could Help

One would assume that people who are quick at making decisions do so because they are better than others at making decisions, because they have somehow learned to do so. But in actuality, these people have, instead, learned to trust their "inner voice" without question or even hesitation. This requires supreme self-confidence and the willingness to be ready to handle any situation that comes up as a result of the decision. So even though there may not be a learning process for quick decision-making there is a certain "science" to it. That "science' involves accessing the information stored in your subconscious.

As I said earlier, invariably in just about every situation, there's a part of us that knows what to do. Perhaps that's because, with our super-computer brains, human beings are able to tap into the "universal intelligence" and gain access to all knowledge, past and present. And even if we are unwilling to believe in such esoteric notions as "universal intelligence", we can be sure that the subconscious mind stores every little bit of information it is ever exposed to and has it all available for lightning speed recall.

But because our education system does not focus on teaching children how to develop their mental powers, focusing instead on the memorization of names, dates, events, etc., we find all kinds of ways to set up obstacles to our intuitive abilities.

In spite of this, it's still safe to say however, that we have all at some point, had an experience wherein stored information from our subconscious has risen up and guided us in making a decision.

Learning to get out of our own way consciously and let the subconscious mind do more of the heavy lifting is a path to much greater, less stressful achievement.

Take Action When You Get The Idea

Another key piece of advice that has served me well over the years is, "Shorten the time between when you get an idea and when you do something to implement it." Make no mistake: there is no wealth in the idea itself; the real wealth is in *acting* on the idea.

Have you ever heard of someone who procrastinated on implementing an idea only to have someone else bring the same idea to the marketplace first? It happens all the time. While one entrepreneur is piddling around trying to get everything perfect before launching his new product or service, the more success-oriented entrepreneur just plows ahead and gets his materials out where people can see and buy them. He follows the philosophy that "Good is good enough."

All too often, people misinterpret this classic piece of advice to mean that you should put any old thing out into the marketplace to try to make some money with it. They completely miss the point that the statement reads, "**GOOD** is good enough" not "Crap is good enough!"

Read another way, this advice can be interpreted as, "You don't have to get it perfect right away but you do have to get it started!"

Taking action (and ideally *massive* action) is an excellent way to breed the confidence that's needed to survive in today's business world. As you become more confident and more skilled you will deliver more and more value to the marketplace, which will inevitably result in your achievement of whatever financial and other goals you may have set for yourself. You will also develop the confidence that it takes to withstand the turmoil that exists in today's business world.

Some of your ideas will be abysmal failures; others will be sure-fire successes. You must develop the stamina and willpower to keep pushing on, no matter which hand is dealt you. All too often your peers, colleagues and even relatives will voice objection to what you may conceive. They'll tell you that you're crazy, that your outlandish ideas will never work. You must learn to ignore them and trust your gut instinct. Then after they are jealous of you and envious of your tremendous success, you must then develop immunity to the criticism that they may inevitably direct at you.

So learn to take action when that little voice, that voice that always knows, speaks to you.

- Dwight Woods

For more information on Dwight Woods, Jeet Kune Do training, martial arts marketing or consulting for small businesses, visit: www.TheJeetKuneDoRebel. com or call: (305) 595-2892, fax: (305) 595-8175, or like him at facebook. com/Dwight D. Woods or send an email to jkdrebel@gmail.com

---

"One of my favorite sayings is: 'what you focus on expands.' So many nowadays focus their energy on what they *don't want* in their lives. Then they have a hard time understanding why they never get what they *do want*. Is it any wonder why?"

- Andrew J. Cass

"I have learned to factor in two inescapable truths into every plan: 1) Nothing will ever go exactly according to plan; and 2) Something will always go wrong in your plan. Fortunately or unfortunately, depending on how you look at it, the only way to discover exactly what it is that will go wrong is to take your plan off the drawing board and out to the real world."

- RJon Robins

"I have found that learning to trust your instincts and develop the courage to follow through quickly on new ideas can mean the difference between getting things done, or not getting them done at all."

- Carlos Castellanos

"For years I fought allowing my 'feelings' to help me make decisions and was labeled many times as being 'too emotional'. It's taken years of conscious work, but now it's much easier to work with these feelings and allow them to guide me."

- Mande White

"A successful leader will attempt to obtain all the logical facts possible and also will learn to trust in their own intuitive instincts in making good decisions."

- Christine Myers

"A sure recipe for success: shorten the time between idea and implementation of idea."

- Dwight Woods

"Successful people can assess a situation and make a decision quickly backed with action. They do not have 'paralysis of analysis.' Sometimes it's a GUT feeling and sometimes it's a BFO (Blinding Flash of the Obvious) that moves a person into action."

- Debbie Wysocki

"There is so much we don't know about the capability of our minds. The realm of what we don't know that we don't know is incomprehensible. Maybe intuition is our ability to include what we don't know into our thinking, combining it with the logic of what we do know."

- John Tate

"In giving your customer or employer all your service, knowledge and quality you have, the awards will be greater than expected."

- Alle van Calker

CHAPTER 10

TAKE ACTION TO PROFIT FROM THE POWER OF POSITIVE ASSOCIATION

By Dan Kennedy and Christine Myers

Advertising agency empire-builder David Ogilvy established a tradition of welcoming new executives with a gift of five wooden dolls, each smaller than the other, one inside the other. When the recipient finally gets to the fifth little doll, the smallest doll, and opens it, he finds this message: *if each of us hires people who are smaller than we are, we shall become a company of dwarfs, but if each of us hires people who are bigger than we are, we shall become a company of giants.*

You can certainly take this beyond hiring. If you surround yourself and spend time with people who are 'smaller' than you are, you will stay as you are.

Take action to involve smart people in your projects. I am constantly impressed with how my clients, Greg Renker and Bill Guthy of the Guthy-Renker Corporation pull together project teams, invite outside experts and consultants to their company meetings, collect qualified opinions and data, and patiently explore differing viewpoints. They constantly apply Napoleon Hill's "mastermind principle."

Take A Millionaire To Lunch

There are smart people readily accessible everywhere. You might seek out and tap retired and highly experienced executives or entrepreneurs in your field to assist and advise you. (SCORE, the Service Corps. Of Retired Executives, under the auspices of the SBA even provides such consultants free to many small businesses.) You might find successful people in your field, in other geographic areas, happy to share their experiences for the price of a lunch or dinner.

My speaking colleague, the late Jim Rohn, urges people: "Take a millionaire to lunch." Jim says to buy him a big juicy steak, fine wine, then dessert and keep asking him questions, and keep listening carefully. And he observes that most people are too shortsighted to ever take this advice; *hey, the guy's a millionaire? – let him buy his own steak.* I'd add that most people take people to lunch who know less than they do, have less successful experience than they do, like a tennis player preferring the company of inferior players.

You might find smart, helpful people through professional associations or at seminars and conferences. You might need to hire smart people to advise you or provide very specialized services for your business. Only one thing is certain; you won't find smart people if you do not take action to find them.

Recently, at the American Booksellers Association (ABA), I ran into a young couple that had authored and published an excellent, unusual travel book. I had met them about 7 months earlier at a conference for self-publishers where I spoke. At that conference, they had asked me a few questions, but been resistant to advice they didn't like, clearly eager for someone to validate their own opinions, and even more clearly unwilling to pay for expert assistance. At ABA, they told me of having just appeared on a major national, network daytime talk show. But their book wasn't in stores and they never got their own 800# given out on the show, were not prepared to negotiate that with the show's producers, and were not prepared to hold their own as one of several guests on a panel – another of the guests monopolized the entire show.

I certainly could have made sure they got their 800# shown and given out on the show, the calls handled, probably sold 5,000 or more books immediately by phone and collected three times that many inquiries, coached them in asserting themselves on the show, and otherwise helped them capitalize on this 'very difficult to get' exposure. And I'm not the only one; there is any number of people very well qualified as advisors in such a situation. But they squandered a once-in-a-lifetime opportunity by being stubborn and by being cheap.

Every business, every occupation and every field has grown far too complex for one person to go it alone and capably handle every aspect of the activity. Insisting on doing EVERYthing yourself is very false economy.

In his first book, Lee Iacocca wrote about his "team of horses" – the mastermind group that turned Chrysler into a winner. In many instances, the existence and importance of a mastermind group within a business or organization goes unnoticed by most of the outside world. But behind most successes, there is between a 2-person and a 20-person mastermind alliance hard at work.

Now, here's a tricky part: you cannot listen only to advice you like and only to opinions that validate your own. Well, you can, but you'll almost certainly fail in most of your endeavors. Sometimes the most valuable person is the one with the courage to confront you and tell you "the Emperor has no clothes."

On the other hand, you need to take great care in choosing those people you test ideas on and solicit opinions from. At my seminars, I all too often hear from the person who had a "great idea", bounced it off a few friends, got talked out of it, only to subsequently see someone else come up with the same idea and go on to amass a fortune. It's a frequently told tale.

In describing the proper makeup of a 'mastermind group' – the short list of those people you choose to routinely serve as your sounding boards – Dr. Napoleon Hill wrote: *"We share nothing we plan to achieve with anyone except those who believe in us and who are in complete sympathy with our plans."* This does not mean "yesers". No, we need good criticism. We need someone to point out the flaws and hazards we may overlook in our enthusiasm. But these people have to be truly eager for our success, confident of our abilities, progressive, innovative and optimistic in general, and possessing of successful, relevant experience and knowledge.

Walt Disney was more brutal and brief in his comments about others' opinions. He would typically ask ten people for their opinions and when all ten disliked one of his ideas he would rate that one as most worthy of investment. The great actor Peter Ustinov said, "If the world should blow itself up tomorrow, the last audible voice would be that of an expert saying: it can't be done."

Beware the expert who can only tell you what you canNOT do (or canNOT do without the expert). Look, instead, for the knowledgeable person who may point out flaws and question premises but can and will also suggest possibilities and improvements and, in general, is eager to figure out how you CAN accomplish your stated objectives.

Such people have to be "big" enough not to be jealous or envious of your success and accomplishments. They have to be smart enough to know what they do not know, and secure enough to admit it – a person with equally strong opinions about everything cannot be trusted. They must not fear the truth or shun reality, but

they must be, overall, optimistic and positive-minded by nature. To paraphrase the title of Peter McWilliams' book, "you cannot afford the luxury of a truly negative individual as a close advisor." And your collection of advisors should include people from 'inside' your particular field and from other, diverse fields as well.

Finally, in soliciting and considering opinions, there is a time to say "enough has to be enough" and then take action. I have often taken pains to correct peoples' picture of the entrepreneur as a 'wild-eyed risk-TAKER', defining the entrepreneur, instead, as someone who MANAGES risk.

Obviously, the more information and worthwhile opinion you can assemble and consider before making an important decision, the better – however this balances out against a value-of-passing-time issue…the assembly and evaluation of information can become a never-ending pursuit in and of itself, with always one more person yet to be heard from, one more source yet to consult, one more piece of data to be obtained. If you're constantly seduced by the next piece of information to be uncovered, 'paralysis of analysis' takes over.

The 3-Legged Stool Of Successful Achievement

Picture in your mind a 3-Legged Stool. If any one leg is missing, you can't sit on it; you topple over. One leg is no more important than the other. All three legs share exactly equal importance. Two without three is no better than one without two or even none. All three are vitally necessary. Their importance is evenly, perfectly balanced. So, one of these legs is: INFORMATION. Another: ADVICE AND ASSOCIATION. The third is: DECISION AND ACTION.

Watch the pro football coach on the sidelines, the next time a game is on television. He has less than a minute between plays, to direct his offense. He has INFORMATION: in his hands, usually on pages attached to a clipboard, is a "game plan", including a collection of planned plays, all built on prior, careful analysis of information collected about the opposing team's strengths, weaknesses and behavior, as well as his own players' abilities, strengths and weaknesses.

He has ADVICE AND ASSOCIATION: during the week before the game, most coaches confer with all their assistant coaches and players, and often by phone with a few trusted, little-mentioned advisors, like other coaches, retired coaches. During the game, he is getting input from assistant coaches in the 'skybox' above the field and from other assistants on the sidelines with him. He is getting instant feedback from the players – "here's what happened"…"here's what I noticed on the last play."

But then he still has less than a minute to arrive at DECISION. And, it doesn't matter whether it is what might be judged as a minimally important situation; the first play of the game; or a life-or-death situation, 4th and 4, two minutes left, down by a touchdown, he still has less than a minute. How would you do under similar pressure?

Of these three legs, ADVICE AND ASSOCIATION is the one you can and need to set up in advance, cultivate over time, and use on a daily basis. You'll do yourself a great favor by organizing your own network, your own "brain trust" or people whose judgment and support you can depend on. You'll do yourself another favor by joining formal mastermind groups and coaching programs run by reputable experts.

The individual who provided this book to you may very well offer such programs. In fact, I'll tell you now that your local Renegade South Florida Entrepreneurs / GKIC Miami Chapter run by our Certified Independent Business Advisor (IBA) and co-author of this book, Andrew J. Cass, is 'The Place' where truly smart, progressive South Florida Entrepreneurs gather monthly to share timely, cutting-edge marketing information and "what's working today" strategies. There is NO other group like this one in South Florida. Bar none. Andrew even offers private mastermind groups and high-level consulting as well for those who qualify.

For more information about the group and to attend an event for FREE visit: www.NoBSMiami.com

- Dan Kennedy

In the words of Christine Myers...

Did you know that being in the right place at the right time is only part of how you can get access to the people you want to meet?

Unless you are willing to seek out and learn from those who are experts in their industries, you can't expect to build your own successful business or career. Every day you're surrounded by opportunities, many of which can be found working or volunteering for non-profits, religious organizations, or other charities.

While organizations such as these rely on the generosity of others, it takes talented executive leaders to transform their teams of dedicated individuals into highly functional and sustainable organizations. I was fortunate to be involved with such an organization, one that took me from being a stay-at-home mom and trained and transformed me into an effective leader in my own right. I organized, implemented, and participated in special events engaging over 600 children at a time, which not only maintained their interests, but also directed their enthusiasm and energies into positive interactions and community involvement. I also had the opportunity to train and manage new and existing adult team members and be actively involved with the scheduling and logistics of teachers and assistants.

One of the most valuable lessons I learned about how to be an effective leader, was the power of the 'Fail Forward' philosophy. To 'Fail Forward' is to change how you think about a perceived failure and turn it into a lesson from which you can learn something valuable and new. It guided my team and I to a better understanding of why certain elements during an event were successful — the good stuff — and how to evaluate and change those things that didn't work. It also taught us how to better respond, rather than react, to any negative situations, issues, or people.

These events also put me in a position to work with the top executives in the organization that I admired and respected; allowing me to align myself with their overall goals and objectives. The added benefit of these experiences gave me the confidence, knowledge, tools, and connections to help me advance in the business world. I also realized that it was my responsibility to be aware of and to take advantage of the excellent resources available to me both in and outside of the workplace.

Unexpected opportunities will often present themselves in the most unlikely places, and you need to be ready to take advantage of them. Also, never underestimate the power of your own capabilities to learn new skills and strategies from others — from in-house training, reading, listening to CDs and teleconferences to attending seminars and workshops — whenever possible, <u>always</u> seek out the best resources. I'll tell you first-hand, by far the best tools for business growth and personal growth I've ever come across are those put out by the GKIC team, here locally and also at the national level.

Identifying where you can meet people who know more than you do is just as important. By joining local and national professional organizations — in your industry and that of your clients — will give you access to other experts while helping you to position yourself as a knowledgeable resource, too. As you align yourself with these experts, you will find you are adding a whole new dimension to your personal learning process.

There are several ways to get to know your fellow members and forge relationships with guest experts who come to speak at an organization's meeting or special event. Three great ways are to join the membership committee, or hospitality committee, or ask to become a member of the organization's board of directors.

During major events, volunteers are always needed to ensure everything runs smoothly. If you want to introduce yourself to the key speakers before everyone else, volunteer to meet and greet them when they arrive or assist them while they are there. If you want to position yourself as a go-to person, help out at the registration desk or information booth. Not only will you have direct access to and face-to-face time with the members and VIPs, but you will also see the list of whose planning to attend before the event. These valuable one-on-one moments will enhance your professional relationships and give you the opportunity to be of service to others at the same time.

Likewise, if you are attending a regional or national event, your sense of camaraderie with those volunteers who greet you will elevate your empathy towards them. Many of the same challenges they are handling, you may have already dealt with previously. Never hesitate to lend a helping hand if there is an immediate need. You never really know how great an impression you will have on someone and how they may be in a greater position to help you later.

Taking it a step further, once you have learned from an expert and tested the lessons yourself, you can then add your perspective and teach others, or use that knowledge to benefit your clients in some added-value way. As you find sources of inspiration, brilliant strategies, and workable solutions; you will become a more valuable resource to others. In doing so, you will further develop and enhance your own sphere of influence by forging these new connections and extending them to like-minded people.

Another aspect of Positive Association is how it helps you find direction and alignment with what rings true with you, so you can follow your passion. Enjoying what you do in a place where you like to be creates a positive experience for yourself and others.

Participating in activities such as mastermind groups and coaching programs can further elevate your aspirations and keep you accountable at the same time. Drawing on the expertise and experiences of others can help you to avoid costly mistakes.

I am reminded of what Timothy Ferriss, the author of *The 4 Hour Work Week* said, *"you are the average of the five people you associate with most, so do not underestimate the effects of your pessimistic, unambitious, or disorganized friends. If someone isn't making you stronger, they're making you weaker."* By taking this advice to heart and examining your current relationships and how they align with your personal and professional goals will help you get a better idea of just whom you want to be with, work with, or be associated with in the long term.

The choice is yours. The more powerful your relationships are with those of like aspirations, the more committed you are to excellence; the more enthusiastic your desire is to learn, the more positive your associations will be.

As the Membership Coordinator for the local Renegade South Florida Entrepreneurs / GKIC Miami Chapter, I invite you to come and associate with a powerful and inspiring group of business owners and entrepreneurs right here in your own backyard.

- Christine Myers

Christine Myers takes the overwhelm out of running a business by providing Virtual Administrative Support to entrepreneurs, business owners and busy professionals. Having those nagging details taken care of allows the business owner the freedom to focus on driving profit and promoting growth in their company. To learn more about the benefits of working virtually, call Christine today, for a Complimentary Consultation at 954-496-6982. For a full list of services, visit her website at www.virtualassistantservices.net

---

"I've been saying for years that 'Association' is the single biggest factor in a person's success. I truly believe it is."

- Andrew J. Cass

"It actually requires more effort to keep the 'time vampires' away than to attract and make connections with action-oriented winners who will be a more positive influence in your life. We know that little hinges swing big doors. So we're always eager to meet and exchange ideas with other action-oriented people."

- RJon Robins

"The Power of Association can't be overstated. My mastermind members and mentors are among my most powerful assets. They see possibilities for me that I myself don't recognize. They push me to break through my self imposed limits."

- Carlos Castellanos

"My 3 legged stool was quite wobbly for years as I was voraciously absorbing all the information and advice that I could. It wasn't until I began working with a coach who helped me take decisive action and held me accountable did I experience catastrophic leaps in my business and my life."

- Mande White

"We don't always have control over what happens to us. We do have a great deal of control over how we prepare ourselves and position ourselves in order to reach our goals. Position yourself for Success."

- Christine Myers

"Repeatedly we hear that even the greatest in their respective fields have coaches upon whom they depend for guidance, peer groups they use for advice and mastermind groups in which they participate for further advancement of their abilities."

- Dwight Woods

"The principle of surrounding yourself with people who are BIGGER than you allows us to grow."

- Debbie Wysocki

"I've seen all too often where advice is asked in regard to a decision and a red flag is thrown up by one of the responders, thus creating a good reason for indecision. A trusted mastermind group that has no ulterior motives can eliminate the need for one to go to unqualified advisors that happen to simply be available at the time."

- John Tate

"When I just started my business I did not market or promote it at all. My association with GKIC taught me how to market and my revenue doubled in a year!"

- Alle van Calker

That may not have been the perfect action...
but at least now he knows you like him.

CHAPTER 11

TAKE ACTION TO (AT LEAST) DOUBLE YOUR PAY CHECK

By Dan Kennedy

Here is the truth no politician, few economists, few teachers want to tell people, and that few people want to hear: certain jobs are only worth a certain, maximum number of dollars per hour, whether you've been there doing it for one year, ten years, or thirty years. Longevity does not necessarily merit more money because the individual's length of time on the job does not necessarily increase the real *value* of getting that job done.

Financial problems of big bureaucracies like the U.S. Postal system, the airline industry, the auto industry…our inability to compete in world markets…quality problems in our educational system….have a lot to do with the pressure on employers to pay more to people purely based on length of time on a job.

Demagogue union leaders and politicians perpetuating this 100% false economy for their own gains have done irreparable harm to this country. Academics who wish to ignore how the economy really works and MUST really work have aided and abetted the fraud committed on the American public on workers, and on students being prepared for careers. The reason France has suffered with a 20% unemployment rate --- yikes! --- for over a decade is this foolish notion that jobs increase in value.

As our economy is forced to acknowledge this uncomfortable reality in the years to come, there will be a great many bitter casualties. <u>However, hidden inside this uncomfortable truth, is the secret to increasing your income literally at will.</u>

In his book, Earl Nightingale's *Greatest Discoveries*, Earl noted that, "every field of human endeavor has its stars; all the rest in these fields are in a descending order of what we might call 'the **service-reward continuum**.' " He went on to point out that the reason some people earn more money than others is that they have made themselves more valuable. He observed that, for the most part, the size of a person's paycheck is determined by this question – *how difficult is he or she to replace?*

As I was writing this, I was listening to a roundtable debate on a Sunday morning news program about employment, productivity and security in America, and a young employee had this question for management and for unions – "How will <u>you</u> help me avoid losing my job in the future?"

Well, you see, that's the wrong question. The unions try hard to protect their turf by answering it, and, as a result, they tell a big lie. Management tries hard to answer it and, as a result, they lie. Government even sticks its nose in and tries to answer it and lies. The only real truthful response is to refuse to answer it at all. What this young man needs to do is go find a full-length mirror, sit down in a chair facing it, stare deeply into his own eyes, and ask himself: "What am *I* going to do to avoid losing my job in the future?" The key words are *"what am I going to do?"* – that is <u>the</u> question.

And here are the extension questions:

1. What am <u>I</u> going to do to increase my value in the marketplace?

2. What am <u>I</u> going to do to demonstrably increase my value to my current employer? (or clients, customers, patients.)

3. What am <u>I</u> going to do to increase my value to prospective future employers?

4. What am <u>I</u> going to do to make myself so valuable that I'm the least likely to be cut, the last to be cut?

Unfortunately, the most common responses are: "I don't have time".... "I can't afford to".... "my employer should".... "the government should".... "Take evening classes and spend my own money? Hey, I already work hard all day. When I come home, I'm tired. And I can't afford to take classes. Besides, if these classes are going to give me skills I'll use on the job, my darned employer oughta pay for them. And I ought to get to take the classes during regular work hours. If I have to go to classes on my time, I should get time-and-a-half. Eric Hoffer wrote, "There are many who find a good alibi far more attractive than achievement."

I have sometimes been introduced, as a speaker, as 'The Professor Of Harsh Reality.' Well, here is the harsh reality every adult should come to grips with as quickly as possible, every young person should be taught: one year, three years, and five years from now, the particular job (task) you do will <u>not</u> have appreciably increased in value. YOU will either have stayed the same in value or increased in value through your own initiative;

that's the only way. If you have not increased in value and your job has not inherently increased in value, at some point, your employer can't or clientele won't pay more — regardless of inflation. It is at that point that your economic status shifts into reverse. Your income stagnates or declines. The gradual decline in your buying power as a consumer will prevent you from saving, investing and creating financial security or erode what you have already accumulated.

And your vulnerability to lay-off, termination or replacement increases. This is true of the self-employed, the business owner, the Entrepreneur, as well. If you are not increasing your value to your customers, if you are not making yourself indispensable to them all over again, every day, then you are declining in value to them. You are either increasing in value or declining in value...

How many people do you thing have this "add value" idea straight in their minds?

...Well, look around. One out of every ten adult Americans is on food stamps. 95% of the people reaching retirement age lack the financial resources to take care of their basic needs without all sorts of direct and disguised welfare. In most big companies, there are masses of people doing the very same jobs, the very same way year after year, even decade after decade, shocked when cheaper foreign labor or automation or some other 'replacement' boots them out on the street. Small business owners suddenly find themselves vulnerable when a major, mass retailer or chain or aggressive new competitor comes to town. How can these terrible things happen to "good people" in America?

Every one of these people has one very distinctive thing in common; from one year to the next, they have not taken any initiative, not done anything, and not invested any money or time in increasing their own personal value. YOU need to look very closely at all these folks and avoid following their example at any and all cost. And if you really would like to double your paycheck, simply take action to triple your value; one of three things will absolutely, certainly happen: 1) your present employer will respond with raises, bonuses and advancement; 2) a new employer will find and grab you; or 3) you'll discover some entrepreneurial opportunity and move on to writing your own paycheck. And if you already own a business and would like to double your paycheck, simply take action to triple your value to your customers. Your compensation will *always* catch up to your value.

- Dan Kennedy

"I'm going to steal a quote already used in this chapter because it's WELL worth repeating: 'There are many who find a good alibi far more attractive than achievement.' Sad but true and, unfortunately, more so today than ever."

- Andrew J. Cass

"I love it whenever any of my employees gets a raise. Every employee should get a raise at least every year. Of course I'm using the word 'get' as an active verb. Whenever an employee asks for a raise I respond, 'give yourself a raise.' "

- RJon Robins

"Freelance artists are notorious for underpricing their work. Reinvention and constant re-evaluation of your value in the marketplace is critical to growing your income."

- Carlos Castellanos

"Playing the entrepreneurial game is the only way I've found to be able to write my own paycheck and pretty much create money on demand. Every time I find ways to increase the value I provide to others, I'm rewarded with more and more income."

- Mande White

"Start thinking about what you can do to help change others' lives for the better. The more value you create in other people's lives, the more money you'll make."

- Christine Myers

"If you have no interest in your own constant, never-ending improvement then you're just taking up valuable space on the planet that someone with more ambition will ultimately occupy, thereby replacing you."

- Dwight Woods

"We are paid for the value we bring to other peoples' lives AND for the size of the problems we solve. Get good at solving peoples' problems."

- Debbie Wysocki

"In the corporate office environment, there is a lot of non-productive time chatting amongst co-workers, personal phone calls, personal email, Internet surfing. Maybe that's just the way it is, but the person that takes it upon themselves to add value back to the employer to make up for this lost time, at a minimum, will rise above the rest."

- John Tate

"Success does not fall into your lap, you have to work and take massive action to make it all happen"

- Alle van Calker

CHAPTER 12

THERE IS NO GREATER POWER

By Andrew J. Cass

W hen I look back at each and every success in my own life, from sports to business to personal, I can always connect it to a *person* or a group of *people* I was associated with that sparked it. Every time. But certainly not just *any* person or group…

The persons and/or groups I've sought out to become involved with over the years were usually way ahead of where I was on the achievement ladder at the time. And I found that the more this was the case, the faster I moved towards success in that given area.

As I mentioned earlier in the book, this was especially true when I was moving further and further into my football career as a young boy in high school and eventually college. By forcing myself into situations in which I was "in over my head," I got myself out of my comfort zone and ultimately, got major <u>results</u>. Well, this also applies as much, <u>if not more</u>, to forcing yourself into relationships and alliances that may appear "over your head"…at first (and usually *only* at first).

So many get this wrong and continue to hang around with the "mediocre majority." So many today love hanging around with people who are _at_ or _below_ the skill or achievement level they are currently at. Why? It's easy. It's comfortable. But then, they wonder why years and years have gone by and not much has changed for them. Not much advancement. No personal growth. No business growth. No financial growth. Just the same stale, stagnant, unfulfilling life.

If this sounds like you, you're not alone. In fact, you're in the majority. BUT... the majority is almost always dead wrong. And they're always last to know. Don't ever forget this. If it weren't true, the majority of the population would be happy, thin, and rich. Look around...

It's the 'minority' that prevails time and time again, and always will... or as Warren Buffet says, "buy when the majority is fearful, sell when the majority is fearless." In other words: _do what the minority is doing to get extraordinary results._

Relationships and alliances with the right people at the right time will make or break you. All the talent in the world won't matter one bit without the right people around you, working for you, or with you, supporting you, and more important... pushing you _outside_ of your comfort zone. It should be called the "uncomfort zone." That's the real _zone_ of achievement.

You might want to read this chapter again. It's very brief, but very valuable. Even though this is not THE "Ultimate Success Secret" contained in this book, I believe it is a close second. There is NO greater power than "the power of people" and the power of your relationships... your Association. It's the chief reason why I've gone into business with the most powerful "people" in the direct marketing and business development world, Dan Kennedy and the GKIC Team.

If you haven't figured it out by now, GKIC is the largest association of independent business owners, entrepreneurs, and sales professionals with a shared, strong interest in exceptionally effective, results driven marketing strategies. No *group of people* like this exists anywhere else in the United States. I've checked.

If you'd like to join us at one of our upcoming events, known here locally as Renegade South Florida Entrepreneurs, in partnership with GKIC, I'd love to meet you in person. I've given you the web site various times throughout this book so that you wouldn't miss it...

In the meantime, I've set aside a "No Strings Attached," 2-Month **FREE Trial** for you to take a test-drive of GKIC membership, which includes the No B.S. Marketing Letter, the most widely read print newsletter in the world for small business owners and entrepreneurs, along with over $600 in FREE business building gifts and pure money making information from Dan Kennedy.

This way you can judge for yourself the value of this "Association" before making any financial commitment. This is an exclusive club for highly qualified, highly motivated, highly determined entrepreneurs and businesspeople. Most likely *you*, if you've read this far...

To claim you FREE Trial, visit: www.GKICFreeGift.com

I hope to meet you in person soon...

- Andrew J. Cass

CHAPTER 13

TAKE ACTION TO PROMOTE YOURSELF AND YOUR IDEAS

By Dan Kennedy and Debbie Wysocki

Today I had lunch with Coach Bill Foster, currently in charge of the entire Southwest Conference (SWC) of college basketball, after a long, incredibly distinguished coaching career. Bill gave the famous Jim Valvano his first coaching job. Bill had a phenomenal tenure at Duke and then at the University of South Carolina. *Esquire Magazine* featured him as "Dale Carnegie on the basketball court", because of his reputation as a powerful motivator. He turned Northwestern's program around. In every case, everywhere Bill went, attendance soared, alumni support increased, and community involvement with the team improved dramatically.

Bottom-line: Bill Foster knows how to fill seats. And that's what we talked about at lunch; what he is now busily doing for the SWC's schools, most with sagging attendance. He is teaching and motivating coaches to become promoters, and he is relentlessly promoting. Last year, the tournament's big Tip-Off Luncheon, for example, had only 300 in attendance; this year, 1,000; and Bill's goal for the next one, 1,500 – a 500% increase in two seasons. Schools with game attendance down to 2,000 will, with a single season, climb to 4,500 with Bill's determined influence.

What Bill Foster Knows About Success That Most People Don't (Or Don't Want To)

Here's what Bill told me, that everybody needs to hear and take to heart (whether they like it or not): "Coaches", he told me, "often don't understand that what they do off the basketball court, all year round, in their communities and with the national media, promoting, is as important as what they do on the court" – because if attendance sags, the university's easiest fix is to fire the coach and bring in a new coach, with new excitement and new promises. Because if attendance sags, recruiting suffers. Because if attendance sags, player confidence and commitment suffers.

In other words, a very, very important part of the coach's responsibility is "promotion." In other words, the "core" of coaching (like the "core" of operating a restaurant, owning a pet shop, writing books, being a jeweler, whatever) is not of sole importance; it is not the key to success. The smart coach is an assertive, creative promoter. One of the signs on my wall says, *"A terrible thing happens when you don't promote,"* Bill said, smiling. *"Nothing."*

I have watched Bill's career closely, both at the University of South Carolina, then at Northwestern, now at SWC, and I'll tell you something; if you didn't know where he was, you could figure it out just by collecting and looking at the promotional literature, the calendars, the newsletters, the mailings of each school. One would stand out above all others. And that's where you'd find Bill Foster.

You see, in EVERY field of endeavor, in ANY field of endeavor, the winners are promoters.

Now, some people will want to argue about how unfair that is. I saw some clown from the ABA on a talk show the other day

blaming the legal profession's disfavor with the public on "those few attorneys who do a lot of advertising." At Arizona State University, the academic in-crowd just about ostracized the professor who turned *"Where There's A Will, There's An 'A'* " into a giant nationwide bestseller, making himself famous and rich along the way. That's all crap. It's jealousy. Ego speaking. Those unwilling to promote are always the biggest, most vocal critics of those successful through promotion. Pick any field and you'll find both. You'll find very vocal critics of promoters. And you'll find tremendously successful promoters.

General Patton was viewed by many of his peers as a shameless, egotistical promoter. Madonna, throughout her career, has been sneered at as a no-talent self-promoter. Brandon Tarkintoff. Donald Trump. Richard Nixon brought himself back from utter, unparalleled disgrace to respected status as an astute elder statesman through an aggressively implemented, thorough strategy of self-promotion. And let's add the adage, *"There have been many statues erected to honor those highly criticized, but very few statues erected to critics"*...

You Only Get To Choose
From Door #1 or Door #2

You really have two choices. You can choose to stick your nose up at the promoters, criticize them and criticize promotion, view it as unseemly, as beneath you, as crass, and stand around grumbling about it. OR you can get good at it and use it to create influence, prominence, prestige, credibility, celebrity, career and financial success. It is your choice.

The coaches Bill works with face these choices. Some of those who choose "Door #1" will lose their current positions and move "down" to smaller schools, and there they may very well find happiness, peace of mind, a "home", and that's okay. Many though, will move "down" and be puzzled and embittered by it. They'll live forever in envy of others they judge to be less qualified, less capable coaches than they are. The world is full of such people.

A few will pick "Door #2". *They'll get the message.* They'll somehow get intellectually and emotionally okay with the way things really are. They'll dig in and learn and adapt and grow. They'll become great promoters. And those are the coaches whose names you and I will know.

This Guy Could Start An Argument In An Empty Room – How Can You Succeed With A Personality Like That?

Buddy Ryan, when Defensive Coordinator at the Chicago Bears, irked head coach Ditka, the owner, and countless others with his braggadocio self-promotion. Then he went on to be head coach in Philadelphia, and, in short order, so aggravated the owner and local media he was fired. Then, as defensive coordinator of the NFL's Houston Oilers, Buddy Ryan lost his cool and got into first, an argument, then a fistfight with the offensive coordinator on the sidelines, during a nationally televised game. His "sin" was shown over and over again during the game and on newscasts, in *Sports Illustrated* and the newspapers, and every pundit said, "Now he'll never get another head coaching job." Many peers, sportswriters and others rejoiced in Buddy's demise. Finally, his big, fat mouth had destroyed his career, as it should.

Nuts. As soon as the season ended, the owner of the Phoenix Cardinals grabbed Buddy Ryan like a drowning man clutching a lifesaver. And Buddy grabbed the mike at the press conference and instantly insulted past coaches, players, the owner, and said, "Well Phoenix, you've *finally* got a winner here." And 20,000 season tickets sold like hotcakes.

Reading what Robert Ringer said about "the Leap Frog Theory" in his book *Winning Through Intimidation* literally changed my life. That's when I first got *the message.* I highly suggest you read the book.

Let me now try and summarize the message...

Waiting around to be discovered, to be recognized, to be noticed, to be appointed, to be promoted, guarantees one thing and one thing only: old age. Focusing on doing whatever it is that you do better than anybody else and trusting that that alone is enough (and arguing tireless that it *should* be enough) guarantees one thing and one thing only: a long life of labor in oblivion.

If Jesus had hung around his hometown working as a carpenter, giving his talks at the local Kiwanis Club meeting, writing books that never got published, waiting to be discovered, we might all be Zen Buddhists today. He was a pretty bold, bombastic promoter. Turned wet bread into fish. Healed the blind. Pitched a fit about the merchants hanging around the temple. Well, you know the story. I don't have to tell you about it. You know the story because Jesus was such a great promoter.

- Dan Kennedy

In the words of Debbie Wysocki...

No matter what the game, the way to win is promotion. I sum it up with this quote... "How you do anything, is how you do everything!"

It took me several years to figure this out – I actually thought my business was about the product. Yes, in order to have integrity, you have to represent a product that you believe in that delivers the results you promise, BUT it's not about the product . . .

It's about YOU solving a need and making sure YOUR name is the one they think of when that need comes to them. Don't you want YOUR company to be the one people think of when they decide to purchase the 'green purple people eater'? It's all about the relationships you create and how you choose to create them. Will you impact people one person at a time? Will you create a movement that can impact 100s or even thousands?

In mentoring my 'Women with Dreams Team', we teach more than 50 ways to market your business both on and offline. I believe if you are going to be a savvy marketer, you want to hit on ALL cylinders, not just half of them. In today's frenzy of Internet marketing, most people don't ever think about traditional marketing. Yes, there is the one in a million success story for Internet Marketers, but how about upping the odds?

If you logically think about where a person spends their time, you'll see what I mean. What is the average number of minutes an average person spends on the computer? According to the United States Department of Labor Survey in 2009 (the latest date for which information was available), women spent approximately 20-25 minutes a day on non-work related computer activities, while men spent 25-40 minutes per day. What is the average number of minutes an Internet Marketer spends on the computer? About 1,000 minutes (in case you're wondering, there's 1,440 minutes in a day)

Obviously a BIG difference.

Don't you like to do business with people you know, like and trust? I know I do. I want to know that the person I fork over my hard earned money to is going to give me their best and that my job is important to them. Your clients want that same warm sense of security from you too!

How do you create this "trust factor?" By creating a relationship. And typically, it begins with promotion. What will give you the biggest benefit? That means the biggest customer list (key word customer, meaning someone who has paid you). So, if you want to reach the average person who spends less than an hour a day on the computer for non-work related activities, what are some of the other ways? There is no better time than to do traditional marketing - traditional marketing that will drive people to your website so you can capture their information:

* Volunteer Work (where your heart is)
* Donate Items with your Logo to Local Charities
* Be a Sponsor for Local Charity Events
* Sponsor a Little League or Youth Football Team in a Neighborhood you want to do business – be involved with the Team and get to know the parents
* City Bus
* Post Cards

* Banners on fields (school, business, etc)
* Banner in the rear window of your car
* Targeted Direct mail
* City Buses (in zip codes you want to work)
* The Practically Perfect Designed Business Card (one people won't throw away)
* Speeches or presentations (lunch and learns)
* Article Marketing
* Press Releases
* A hard copy Christmas Card, preferably with a picture of you and your family with an update about your year (let your customers and potential customers get to know you)
* A calendar planner or journal
* Write a Book
* Book Marks
* Tele-Classes
* Webinars
* Professor at a Local Community College
* Be the Expert for your Industry
* Customer Loyalty Program
* Customer Referral Program
* Joint Venture Programs (these really bring gigantic value to your customers)

And so much more!

What items will keep your company front and center in the mind of your customers and potential customers minds? There is a fine line between shameless and obnoxious. I look for an opportunity to put the name of my company, "Women with Dreams," in everything I do, but I never solicit people. I attract people.

Here's a few examples: People see my shirts with the logo, they see my car, and they see the banners on the field at the school my kids go to, and they wonder how I have so much free time – it's the lifestyle. So they naturally ask what I do, which opens the door to conversation.

Of course, you need to track what gets you the best results. You must repeat (test/re-test) your marketing efforts enough to measure the results and determine the best six to seven 'irons in the fire' that you want to focus on. I recommend to my team they have a core of four to five 'irons' and that they test two to three new ways of marketing and <u>promoting</u> regularly.

Don't wait to jump in even if you don't have all the facts. Les Brown says "if it's worth doing, it's worth doing wrong." For most people, if they wait till they have everything perfect, it will never get done. And, I've noticed, most people WAIT. They are too worried about making the right decision or worse, making a mistake. A trait I've noticed about entrepreneurs is they evaluate the facts they have, do reasonable research (no, they do not check into every possible scenario), and then they make a decision. If it's the wrong decision, they adjust.

If you represent a company that has a lot of advertising and marketing rules, you may appreciate my philosophy, "it's better to ask for forgiveness than to ask for permission." Just about nothing gets done when you ask for permission.

How do you bring value to your community, to everyone you come in contact with? When people leave you, do they feel better than when they arrived?

If you can identify the *value* you bring, if people give you positive testimonies, you know you are doing the right activities. So, the big question to ask yourself is, "Am I promoting my business to the best of my ability?" Or, is there something else I could be doing?

In your marketing and promotion, let people feel great about the deal they got. That includes giving bonuses that are unbelievable and valuable. In person, let people know that they matter. Look them in the eye when you talk to them and be present – they will remember you. Let them know they are appreciated. Treat your customers and potential customers the way you would want to be treated. Make sure your name is the first one people think of when they think of your product or any product related to what you do. You want a "community" where your customers will be your best promotion because of the great value you have brought them...

- Debbie Wysocki

Debbie is the founder of Women with Dreams, residual Money secrets (for guys), and the Newly launched 'Women with Dreams MLM Academy' for professional women in Network Marketing who want to create a *Life They Love*. For more information, visit   www.WomenWithDreamsMLMAcademy. com to receive your FREE weekly eNewsletter subscription to: "The Secret Edge for MLM Women - Insider Secrets to Building a Profitable

Business in Today's New Economy." Plus, you'll also receive a complimentary audio, "How To Choose the Right Home Business for You."

"Those who struggle the most promote the least. It's like 1 + 1 = 2. Many say they 'don't have time' to promote. I say you don't have time <u>not</u> to promote."

- Andrew J. Cass

"If you truly believe you product or service helps make your customers' or clients' lives better then you are doing them a disservice by not helping them learn as much as possible about what it is that you have to offer. If you don't believe your products and/or services helps your customers or clients, then fix it."

RJon Robins

"Artists by nature are not promoters. We often work in solitude and most are introverts. However, learning to promote yourself is as critical to your success as is your art."

- Carlos Castellanos

"It's not enough to become a master of your craft if you want to profit handsomely. You must also become a master of copywriting, persuasion, selling and marketing... promotion."

- Mande White

"If you think that the 'doing' of your thing is more important than the marketing / promotion of your thing, then you will not be doing your thing for that much longer. Watch out!"

- Dwight Woods

"If you really believe in the value of your product or service then you owe it to the world to let them know about it."

- Christine Myers

"You can be really great at what you do, but without promotion, no one else will know that you're great. Get the message out. Always do your very best. Get testimonies, and promote, promote, promote."

- Debbie Wysocki

"When promoting an idea or accomplishment, I think using the term 'we' instead of 'I' can turn around a statement that could be interpreted as bragging. It is often more accurate, too."

- John Tate

"Unfortunately I hear it over and over again from employers and business owners that I know. People want to have a job, but they do not want to work… Success does not fall into your lap, you have to work and take massive action to make it all happen"

- Alle van Calker

CHAPTER 14

THE ONLY RELIABLE PATH TO MAXIMUM SUCCESS

By Dan Kennedy and John Tate

M y once speaking colleague, the late Jim Rohn, says that when you look closely at the highly successful individual in any field, you walk away saying to yourself: *"It's no wonder he's doing so well... look at everything he's doing."* Well, there's a darned good test! If we followed you around for a week and painstakingly recorded how you spent your time, what you did every day to advance your career or business, would we wind up saying to ourselves "It's no wonder he's doing so well – look at everything he's doing"?

The truth is that most people are intellectually lazy, surprisingly uncurious in their acquisition of information. And, in their businesses, they lazily rely on only one, two or three methods of attracting customers or clients. As a consultant, quite frankly, I do not walk away from most clients saying, "It's no wonder he's doing so well look at everything he's doing." Mostly, I say to myself: "It's a miracle he's doing as well as he is – look at how <u>little</u> he's doing."

I once knew a chiropractor who built three different million dollar a year practices. Not one, three. Dr. S. built and sold one, moved to another community, built and sold another one. One's a fluke but three's a system, so the word spread and a whole lot of doctors wanted to know how he did that. So many, so much so, that thousands each paid $30,000.00 to come and hear him expound on his methods in seminars. But the essence of his success was really quite simple. Invariably, every doctor asked him the same question:

"How can I get __ new patients this month?" How can I get 30 new patients this month? How can I get 50 new patients this month? The number varied but the question was always the same. And so was Dr. S.'s answer: *"I don't know one way to get 30 new patients, but I know 30 ways to get one new patient and I use every single one of them."*

See, if you need new clients for your business, don't do one thing, do a dozen things. If you have a problem to solve, don't implement one possible solution; implement a dozen. One of the speakers I appeared with frequently during my speaking days is Reverend Robert Schuller, and he's become famous for his story of how he faced the massive cost overruns in completing The Crystal Cathedral. Confronted with a need for ten million dollars, he made a list of ten different ways he might raise that money. Then he went to work on all ten <u>simultaneously</u>.

Take action to <u>diversify</u> the way that money and success comes to you, the way that you solve problems, even the way that you acquire new information and grow as a person.

Curiosity, incidentally, is a wonderful thing. Forget the old 'curiosity killed the cat' thing; curiosity is what uncovers opportunities and makes people rich. The average child of 5 to 10 asks hundreds of questions a day; the average adult asks only a handful. This is why kids have so much energy and enthusiasm for living. This is also why adults age prematurely and rapidly. Life-force itself comes from curiosity and creativity. *"Always Be Creating and Discovering, with Enthusiasm."* When it becomes "went there, did that", you have at least one foot in the grave.

What Kind Of Action Yields The Greatest Results?

Yes, there is one type or kind of "action" that produces maximum results in a minimum length of time, thanks in part to 'the principle of momentum.' Again, it's from Jim Rohn that I first heard about the incredibly powerful Principle Of Massive Action. The key word here is: <u>Massive.</u>

Not tiny action. Not wimpy action. Not tentative action. Not toe-in-the-water action. Not ponderously slow action. Massive action.

In 1946, a man named Walter Russell had his philosophies published, largely because he was such an unusual, larger-than-life figure. Russell never went past elementary school, and his first job was a clerk in a dry goods store earning $2.50 a week. To the amazement of just about everybody who knew of his "non-background", Russell achieved considerable fame and success as an architect, sculptor, and artist. With the publication of his success philosophies, Russell became known as "the man who tapped the secrets of the universe." Russell insisted that every man has consummate genius within and he taught, "every successful man or genius has three particular qualities in common, and the most conspicuous of these is that they all produce a prodigious amount of work."

In his classic *Lead The Field* recordings, Earl Nightingale told, with slight sarcasm, of the man who arrives home everyday and says to his family "Boy am I tired" --- because that's what he heard his father say everyday when he arrived home from work, at a job, under conditions that really warranted the expression of exhaustion. I am often impressed at how little work people are willing to do in order to get what they insist they want.

Let me give you an example of the Principle Of Massive Action *in action:* a woman, Barbara L., cornered me at a seminar, introduced herself as the CEO of a specialized, industrial company – in her words, "a woman in a man's world", and told me of her frustrations and woes with finding financing. She was literally turning away lucrative manufacturing contracts because she couldn't finance the necessary raw materials, labor and other costs while in production and then waiting to be paid a month or so following delivery.

Having once run a specialty manufacturing company with similar problems, I instantly had empathy --- and ideas --- for her, but first I asked some questions. And I was not surprised to discover that she had tried most local banks, suffered rejection, and pretty much given up.

From my own experience, I knew Barbara had stopped at only scratching the surface of potential solutions. But she was no different than most. Most people, confronted with a problem, think of and try only a few solutions, and give up quite easily. This, incidentally, is the blunt truth behind many of our popularized societal ills and failures. Most people who "can't" get jobs actually have given up on getting a job. People who "can't" get off welfare have truthfully given up getting off of welfare. Here's why this is inarguably true: because there are people just like them who have persevered and gotten jobs, who have persevered and gotten off welfare. If one can, <u>everyone</u> can.

So, just as example, here was my prescription for Barbara:

1. Strengthen the proposal package and re-contact every bank that said no. Then keep re-contacting them and bringing them up-to-date every thirty days.

2. Reach out to friends, associates, community contacts, and vendors in search of recommendations of other lenders and/or somebody who has a relationship of some kind with someone of authority in one of those banks.

3. Discuss different formats for the financing: revolving receivables credit line OR asset-based long term loan OR 90-day notes. Ask the banks for different things.

4. Contact banks outside the local market…draw a 300 mile circle around the plant and contact every bank in that circle.

5. Consider a sale/leaseback arrangement with a leasing company for all the equipment and furniture in the factory and offices.

6. Contact the SBA. Through the SBA, get put in touch with SBA Certified Lenders. And investigate the SBA's preferred lending services for women-owned businesses.

7. Get free help through the SBA, from SCORE (Service Corps. Of Retired Executives) for beefing up the business plan, proposal, etc.

8. Meet with key vendors and discuss creative, extended terms that could equate to the same effect as a loan or credit line. Simultaneously, open up conversations with new, alternative vendors who might use credit as a means of acquiring new business.

9. Consider factoring some receivables. Meet with factoring companies and brokers.

10. Offer customers a significant discount for paying 50% to 100% of the contracts in advance. (There is a cost of financing, no matter how you do it. You can convert that cost to a discount for prepayment without impact on true, net profit.)

11. Advertise for private lenders and "angels."

12. Form a new limited partnership or corporation with private investors, which will serve as a financing-for-profit business, lending against your other company's receivables.

13. Franchise or pseudo-franchise exclusive sales territories, and use the fees collected from that to establish your own financing fund.

14. Alter the nature of your business, the "mix" of your business, so you can get cash-with-order business.

15. Through blind, confidential advertising put the entire business up for sale and test the waters.

16. Meet with key employees and discuss possibilities for assembling receivables financing or equity investment from employees.

Now, here's the "trick" I shared with Barbara: do all 16 of these things at the same time. Right now. Fast.

Back when I ran a company with its nose pushed up against this same wall, I did all 16 of these things. In our case, we succeeded with #'s 3, 5, 8, 10 and 14. #10 alone, incidentally, dramatically altered the company's cash flow situation, even though everybody told me that the clients in our industry would never pre-pay for their manufacturing orders. In three months, we converted over half the existent clients to pre-paying, for a 10% discount.

But if we had tried one, done everything we could before giving up on one, THEN tried two, done everything we could with two, THEN tried three… it's pretty obvious that time's going to win and we're going to lose.

Of course, she might have responded – as most would – with "Geez, that's a lot of work!" And she might have said, "How am I supposed to get all that done?"… and… "But I don't know how to do all those things?"… or … "I'll be working until midnight everyday to do all that." Etc. But I'm delighted to report that Barbara found an SBA Certified Lender-bank, secured a long-term loan replacing all her other financing and providing expansion capital, and she found three private individuals happy to finance individual, large receivables from new contracts as she needs them. And, it's no wonder Barbara finally got her financing; look at everything she did!

Could You Cultivate THE Most Prized Personal Characteristic Of Any And All Known To Man?

Let me give you one other example that leads us to, yet another important success behavior… In Fort Wayne, Indiana, for me, disaster struck. Years ago the set-up crew for the "Success 94" seminar tour called me in my hotel room, the afternoon before the event, to tell me that none of my product was at the convention center. Everyone at my office's end then did everything they thought they could do to correct the problem, to get UPS to deliver early the next day, to try and trace the location of the shipment. They did everything they *thought* they could do, but they still stopped short of doing everything that *could* be done. As concerned and earnest as they were, they stopped short.

Why? Because very, <u>very</u> few people understand the idea of refusing to accept anything less than success.

After they gave up, I dug in. Through a series of phone calls and conversations, **I** finally got the guy standing on the right receiving dock, in Ft. Wayne, Indiana. I sold him – and I mean: *sold* --- on getting up early the next morning, getting to his warehouse, and going through the carloads of boxes left there during the night to find mine. And to call me by 7:00 AM that morning with the good news that he had done so. And, a little after 7:00 AM, he was on the phone. And he had the boxes loaded in his own, personal pick-up truck. And he brought them to the convention center, undoubtedly in violation of a handful of company regulations.

And, for you cynics, I didn't offer him money, he never asked for money, and when we finally tried to give him money that morning, he refused it. Now, I honestly believe that I did not do anything here that anybody else couldn't have done. This was not a matter of "talent." I just refused to accept anything less than success. I stayed at it long enough and hard enough that I got a little "earned luck", and found a guy like me – two people who can and will "carry the message to Garcia."

If you don't know the story of the man who carried *"A Message To Garcia"*, I've included the story in its actual form below. It reveals the most prized characteristic on earth…

- Dan Kennedy

A Message To Garcia

In all this Cuban business there is one man stands out on the horizon of my memory like Mars at perihelion.

When war broke out between Spain and the United States, it was very necessary to communicate quickly with the leader of the Insurgents. Garcia was somewhere in the mountain vastness of Cuba – no one knew where. No mail or telegraph message could reach him. The President must secure his cooperation, and quickly.

What to do!

Someone said to the President, "There is a fellow by the name of Rowan who will find Garcia for you, if anybody can." Rowan was sent for and given a letter to be delivered to Garcia. How the "fellow by the name of Rowan" took the letter, sealed it up in an oilskin pouch, strapped it over his heart, in four days landed by night off the coast of Cuba from an open boat, disappeared into the jungle, and in three weeks came out on the other side of the Island, having traversed a hostile country on foot, and delivered his letter to Garcia – are things I have no special desire now to tell in detail.

The point that I wish to make is this: McKinley gave Rowan a letter to be delivered to Garcia. Rowan took the letter and did not ask, "Where is he at?" By the eternal! There is a man whose form should be cast in deathless bronze and the statue placed in every college of the land. It is not 'book-learning' young men need, nor instruction about this and that, but a stiffening of the vertebrae, which will cause them to be loyal to a trust, to act promptly, concentrate their energies; do the thing; "Carry a message to Garcia."

General Garcia is dead now, but there are other *Garcias*. No man who has endeavored to carry out an enterprise where many hands were needed, but has been well-nigh appalled at times by the imbecility of the average man – the inability or unwillingness to concentrate on a thing and do it.

Slipshod assistance, foolish inattention, dowdy indifference, and half-hearted work seem the rule, and no man succeeds unless by hook or crook or threat he forced or bribes other men to assist him; or mayhap, God in His goodness performs a miracle and sends him an Angel of Light for an assistant.

You, the reader, put this matter to a test: you are sitting now in your office – six clerks are within call. Summon any one and make this request: "Please look in the encyclopedia and make a brief memorandum for me concerning the life of Correggio."

Will the clerk quietly say, "Yes, sir," and go do the task?

On your life, he will not. He will look at you out of a fishy eye and ask one or more of the following questions:

Who was he? Which encyclopedia? Where is the encyclopedia? Was I hired for that? Don't you mean Bismarck? What's the matter with Charlie doing it? Is he dead? Is there any hurry? Shan't I bring you the book and let you look it up yourself? What do you want to know for?

And I will lay you ten to one that after you have answered the questions and explained how to find the information, and why you want it, the clerk will go off and get one of the other clerks to help him try to *find Garcia* – and then come back and tell you there is no such man. Of course, I may lose my bet, but according to the Law of Average, I will not.

Now, if you are wise, you will not bother to explain to your "assistant" that Correggio is indexed under the C's, not in the K's, but you will smile very sweetly and say, "Never mind," and go look it up yourself. And this incapacity for independent action, this moral stupidity, this infirmity of the will, this unwillingness to cheerfully catch hold and lift – these are the things that put pure Socialism so far into the future. If men will not act for themselves, what will they do when the benefit of their effort is for all?

A first mate with knotted club seems necessary; and the dread of getting "the bounce" Saturday night holds many a worker to his place. Advertise for a stenographer, and nine out of ten who apply can neither spell nor punctuate – and do not think it necessary to.

Can such a one write *a letter to Garcia*?

"You see that bookkeeper," said the foreman to me in a large factory.

"Yes, what about him?"

"Well, he's a fine accountant, but if I'd send him uptown on an errand, he might accomplish the errand all right, and on the other hand, might stop at four saloons on the way, and when he got to Main Street would forget what he had been sent for."

Can such a man be entrusted to carry *a message to Garcia*?

We have recently been hearing much maudlin sympathy expressed for the "downtrodden denizens of the sweatshop" and the "homeless wanderer searching for honest employment," and with it all often go many hard words for the men in power. Nothing is said about the employer who grows old before his time in a vain attempt to get frowzy ne'er-do-wells to do intelligent work; and his long, patient striving after "help" that does nothing but loaf when his back is turned.

In every store and factory, there is a constant weeding out process going on. The employer is constantly sending away "help" that have shown their incapacity to further the interests of the business, and others are being taken on. No matter how good times are, this sorting continues: only, if times are hard and work is scarce, the sorting is done finer – but out and forever out the incompetent and unworthy go. It is the survival of the fittest. Self-interest prompts every employer to keep the best – those who can carry *a message to Garcia.*

I know one man of really brilliant parts who has not the ability to manage a business of his own, and yet who is absolutely worthless to anyone else because he carries with him constantly the insane suspicion that his employer is oppressing or intending to oppress him. He cannot give orders, and he will not receive them. Should a message be given to him, *to take to Garcia,* his answer would probably be, "Take it yourself!"

Tonight this man walks the streets looking for work, the wind whistling through his threadbare coat. No one who knows him dare employ him, for he is a regular firebrand of discontent. He is impervious to reason, and the only thing that can impress him is the toe of a thick-soled Number Nine boot.

Of course, I know that one so morally deformed is no less to be pitied than a physical cripple; but in our pitying let us drop a tear, too, for the men who are striving to carry on a great enterprise, whose working hours are not limited by the whistle, and whose hair is fast turning white through the struggle to hold in line dowdy indifference, slipshod imbecility, and the heartless ingratitude which, but for their enterprise, would be both hungry and homeless.

Have I put the matter too strongly? Possibly I have; but when all the world has gone a slumming, I wish to speak a word of sympathy for the man who succeeds – the man who, against great odds, has directed the efforts of others, and having succeeded, finds there's nothing in it; nothing but bare board and clothes. I have carried a dinner-pail and worked for day's wages, and I have also been an employer of labor, and I know there is something to be said on both sides.

There is no excellence, per se, in poverty; rags are no recommendation; and all employers are not rapacious and high-handed, any more than all poor men are virtuous. My heart goes out to the man who does his work when the "boss" is away, as well as when he is at home. And the

Who, when given *a letter for Garcia*, quietly takes the missive, without asking any idiotic questions, and with no lurking intention of chucking it into the nearest sewer, or of doing naught else but deliver it, never gets "laid off," nor has to go on a strike for higher wages.

Civilization is one long, anxious search for just such individuals. Anything such a man asks shall be granted. He is wanted in every city, town and village - in every office, shop, store and factory. The world cries out for such; he is needed and needed badly – the man who can *"Carry a Message to Garcia."*

In the words of John Tate...

I was fortunate enough during my early twenties to have a near death experience. I was thrown from the back window of a fifteen passenger Dodge Caravan when a tire blew out on the highway and left me with two collapsed lungs and paralyzed from the neck down. With many great people assisting (thank you paramedics onsite almost immediately and my neurosurgeon Dr. Rodts), I was able to walk again within four weeks.

I would not trade that experience for anything...

While lying in the hospital bed I came to the realization that it is my duty to make the most out of my life and there was no reason I couldn't reach any peak of accomplishment. The short, yet very rich thought that came to mind was, "Why *Not* Me?" Meaning, "Why shouldn't I be the one to achieve great things?" And "why shouldn't I have absolutely anything I want in the world?"

I still use that phrase today. If I have a momentary thought that something is not in my league or just reserved for others it is quickly banished by, "Why not me?" This little phrase is gold to me and is the only reason I need to take massive action.

The near-death experience and resulting phrase likely played a large part in my leaving five different six-figure income jobs in order for a chance at something more...stock options, equity, my own business. There were many times along the way when I thought, "What have I done?" After all, I have a family to support so maybe it is irresponsible of me to be taking these actions. But I have marched on, and things do seem to work out with persistence.

The greater the struggle, the greater the return will be in the end...

A friend of mine and I tell each other when things are bleak that, "this will make it an even better story". So true, right? It would be a shame to accomplish much in life, millions of dollars, homes, fancy cars, and then not be able to tell a great story about how you were skimming bottom and then be able to detail the rough times before persistence brought you the deserving success. Beats the heck out of, "I won the lotto." In fact, that is a reason why I don't play the lottery... I don't want to win. What fun would that be? No long hard road. No struggle. Nope... to me it would feel a bit empty, no matter how much good I might be able to do with that money.

I will have started with nothing, found success (in others minds maybe) several times, had nothing again, and risen. Much better story I think. But it all begins with massive action. This takes effort. There is no way around that. Sacrifices by all, including those who love you.

I recall one specific instance in my life that induced my entrepreneurial ways. It began when I read a book you've likely heard of (one of the best selling entrepreneurial books of last 10 years) called "Rich Dad, Poor Dad". This book did something to me... it awakened my entrepreneurial spirit. I had not been aware of this spirit in me previously, but it took hold and hasn't relinquished to this day. If you haven't read it, it is about a boy that grows up with both an education-focused father and a friend's father who is a very successful self-made entrepreneur. The book brings forward the value of creating an entity that pays you while you sleep, while you are vacationing in Europe, or doing anything else other than collecting a check for showing up or being paid by the hour.

I had always been paid as an employee, and although well paid, I was sure they *would not* continue to pay me if I didn't produce good work on a daily basis for them. I was not driven by the thought of getting paid for doing nothing, because I do appreciate tough tasks and overcoming obstacles, but I was certain that to become whomever I thought I was capable of becoming would involve the independence of doing it on my own. So I became a student again. Not by getting an MBA. Nothing against that (as this was the path I had been planning), but I felt like I needed more specialized training. I began reading about how to properly value a business, since it occurred to me that possibly purchasing a business was the way to become an entrepreneur, since I hadn't yet had an idea for one.

While undergoing this education, I took a great course called "How to Buy a Good Business at a Great Price". This course was a wealth of knowledge, and I was so impressed by it I contacted the author, Richard Parker. He happened to also live in South Florida (coincidentally), so inquired with him if there were anything that we might be able to work on together, although to this point, my only expertise was in consulting, project management, software implementation, and account management. He didn't think so, but was very nice to me.

Within one month, we were in business together. Together with a close friend, we made a proposal to Richard to turn his course into an online application that would not only provide training, but would perform the calculations, valuations, business plans, and organize all of the information that was required for each business analysis. My friend and I worked tirelessly many nights a week and during the weekends for several months designing the product in detail.

Upon the software development completion and our proposed "go-live", I left my current employer. There...that was my first massive action. Did it work out? No, not directly. The revenue did not come in the quantity that would provide all of the partners with significant enough payout along with replacing my own six-figure income. Although the software is still live with a customer base, I was forced to find something else...and do so quickly!

I think we are all going to fail more than we succeed. Most of the great men of our American history had repeated and significant failure prior to achieving success. George Washington, Abraham Lincoln, Thomas Edison, Franklin Roosevelt and Henry Ford all come to mind. Although failure is embarrassing and might put us into very tight positions, we will come out ahead no matter what. NOTHING teaches like failure.

I have also experienced a failure at bringing a product to retail. I learned a very important lesson from this experience...no matter how great a product is, unless you can easily communicate to its market what the product is and does (and do this prior to being on the retail shelf), it is going to be extremely difficult to find success with a new, never-before seen product.

The product I developed had seemingly everything going for it, from articles in the New York Times, Popular Science, Family Circle to becoming a featured product in *O Magazine's* O-List. The product was a highly secure and encrypted device that made it very easy to store all of your most important personal records and then use it on any computer, wherever you were at the time. We were able to gain prominent space at two of the top three retailers in the country and even had an accompanying video explaining the features at one of the retailers, but it just didn't cut it. The overwhelming lesson I took away from this experience is that you have to take it upon yourself to drive the demand *through* marketing.

Many new products are launched on TV, but the economics have to be just right to make this work and if you have a lot of engineering and pricey components within a product this might not be an option. If you leave the crucial task of driving demand to anybody else- retailers, distributors, *anyone else*, then its chance of significant success is small.

These failures initiated my yearning to learn how effective Internet marketers were able to harness the power of the Internet so profitably. So the second educational phase I initiated involved learning from those that made millions marketing online with little to no overhead. I was determined to bring those same techniques to small businesses and be able to effectively market products or services using the Internet.

The easiest way to reach prospective customers *that are already searching for your type of product or service* is through the Internet. It is a fact that people are now searching for an item they want online before purchasing the product or service (offline or online). As the saying goes, "perception is reality". If people are searching online for products, then we can say that the Internet can form perception, correlating that we can affect reality by what is perceived by prospects while searching online. So why not perform the activities that will form this perception?

The perception could be that a product completely dominates a particular category. Or the perception could be that your company is an industry leader or that more people are talking about your product than any other competitor. This perception can now be manufactured by the little guy through the Internet, and does not require hundreds of thousands of dollars to spend on a product launch or big advertising campaign. One just needs to know how to channel this online power so that it is a cost effective strategy to take your product to the market. This can be done on the national level and is even easier on the local market.

Here is an example of putting my newfound marketing knowledge to use for the launch of a product on a national level...

We were rolling out a new B2B technology product in a newly spun off company. So much money was spent in product development and certifications that marketing needed to be accomplished on a shoe-string budget. We turned to two main ways to get this done, PR and the Internet. Since the product was a completely different solution to a problem, unique, and solved issues that were big topics (data security), we hired a PR firm to make sure that pertinent publications knew about it. But we needed a hub, so we created a website and focused on a small set of phrases (keywords) that we analyzed and figured out that if we developed enough good content (articles, videos, PR, white papers) that we could fairly quickly achieve good Google rankings.

There was an additional issue to conquer...

The product was not yet ready to ship! But creating awareness through PR and driving people already looking for our *product type* to our website, this product that had a lot to overcome, was able to create a huge list of interested organizations, including many Fortune 500 companies, that purchased the product immediately upon its availability.

Fear. It is a dangerous thing. Not *what* we are afraid of, but fear itself. Well, now that sounds a bit like JFK (sorry for the plagiarism) but anyway, fear keeps us from taking risks. Sometimes fear is helpful and can save our life if there is a potentially life threatening situation I suppose, but it mostly acts like a brick wall when it comes to taking action. We tend to get very caught up in thinking about what other people might say about us or to us if we take a large massive action or risk. But maybe the best thing to do in these cases when considering whether to take this risk or not is to think about what is the absolute worst thing that can happen if you fail?

If you were to document this and think about it thoroughly, it likely isn't that bad. Maybe you lose your investment and your family and friends might think less of you. Will you be out on the streets? Will your family be without food or clothing? If you still answer "no" to these two questions, then congratulations, you will still be better off than a large percentage of the population. So the worst is on the table and you still have your health, food and shelter (even if it means living in a cramped apartment or with family temporarily). Worried about failing and not finding another job? Don't! People that take massive action are quickly snapped up and hired by businesses the moment they become available. I'm sure Rowan had no trouble getting work after looking for Garcia.

- John Tate

John Tate helps small businesses promote their business through the power of PR. Public Relations has the unique ability to position clients as expert authorities in their industry or region, while driving prospects and reducing the length of the typical sales cycle. His company, PR Machine, developed a *Hybrid PR* approach that combines traditional PR services with Internet marketing activities to deliver small businesses a much higher ROI.

To see if *Hybrid PR* might be a fit for your business, take the 2-minute quiz at www.prmachine.co or contact John directly at jtate@prmachine co.

"Dan said in this chapter: 'I am often impressed at how little work people are willing to do in order to get what they insist they want.' I'd like to replace the word impressed with the word *dumbfounded*."

- Andrew J. Cass

"In order to provide any measure of pro bono services every sensible business owner knows, it's first necessary to run one's business at a profit."

- RJon Robins

"Admittedly, I have struggled in taking massive action on personal projects. But I continue to invest in myself to improve in this area."

- Carlos Castellanos

"Love this chapter! It's all so true. Sometimes its exhausting to keep so many balls in the air but at least your odds of having something work out are better than if you put all your eggs in one basket. This is not an area I choose to gamble in."

- Mande White

"Unfortunately much in our education system teaches sequential rather than simultaneous. We go from Pre-K to Kindergarten to 1st Grade, 2nd

Grade and so on. Breaking free of such limited thinking can be a major step towards achieving more, more quickly."

- Dwight Woods

"Relentless pursuit is essential to your success. Never! Never! Give Up!"

- Christine Myers

"If you can ask yourself these questions and feel good about the answers: What Did I Do Today? Is there anythingelse I can do before I go to bed that will make a difference in my TOP 3 goals? Then your business will soon be exploding, if it's not already. Why? Because you are taking MAXIMUM ACTION when you are consistently working towards you TOP goals."

- Debbie Wysocki

"Who cares more? The answer to this question often points to the person more apt to 'get it done'."

- John Tate

"Failure is doing the same thing over and over again and expecting a different result. If you can't reach your desired result change the way how you want to get there but do not change the desired result."

- Alle van Calker

CHAPTER 15

TAKE ACTION AND TURN FAILURE INTO SUCCESS

By Dan Kennedy

I once saw a particularly ornery dog latch onto a mailman's leg. The mailman shook his leg but the dog held on, growling menacingly. The mailman kicked the dog with his other leg. The dog held on. The mailman drug the dog down the sidewalk. The dog held on. The mailman sprayed the dog with Mace. He hit the dog on the head with his mail sack. He swung his leg, dog attached, into a tree trunk. The dog held on. I thought to myself: there is the dog version of Dan Kennedy.

In his best-selling book, *Swim With The Sharks,* Harvey MacKay tells of being turned down by all his local lending institutions. Then he drew a 3-inch circle on the map around his city and called on all the banks within that circle. They all turned him down too. He drew a bigger circle. Eventually he got his loan. He says he'd still be drawing ever-bigger circles if he hadn't connected. I believe him.

If you look at most highly successful entrepreneurs, you won't find markedly superior talent, intelligence, education or resources. Self-made millionaires are surprisingly ordinary – and, often, surprisingly unintelligent – people. Conversely, a small percentage of Mensa members are self-made millionaires. So it ain't intelligence. Instead it seems to have much to do with a profound sort of stubbornness...

How You Deal With Failure Determines Whether Or Not You *Ever* Get To Deal With Success

Research supervised by a professor at Tulane University revealed that the average entrepreneur goes through 3.8 failures before achieving significant success.

Actually, the entire entrepreneurial experience is one of frequent failure interrupted by occasional success. The entire experience of selling is one of frequent refusal (rejection) interrupted by occasional acceptance. In direct marketing, we call it "testing", not failure. But a whole lot more "tests" fail than succeed.

Go Ahead, Screw Up. Fall Down. Embarrass Yourself. A Lot. Fast.

There IS value in making mistakes. General Schwarzkopf discussed one situation he encountered where, if a bundle of decisions were made and actions taken and 49% turned out wrong, everybody'd still be way ahead of where they were with no decisions being made and no actions taken. I say: screw up. Fall down. The opposite requires living in constant fear of error, and that's a sad, pitiful existence. You have to look at every significant accomplishment as the end result of a certain number of successes but also a certain number of failures.

At one time, Billy Crystal was one of Hollywood's hottest comic commodities. *City Slickers* was a huge hit, birthing a sequel. But let's not forget his movie *Mr. Saturday Night,* which he deeply believed in, which was 'Dead On Arrival' at the theaters, and which was a huge disappointment to him personally. Everybody, at every level, who is attempting much of anything screws up and falls down.

I watched the great actor from *Cheers,* Ted Danson, on The David Letterman Show once. Danson took his lumps from Letterman about his much-publicized relationship with Whoopi Goldberg, most memorable for Danson's appearance at her Friars Club Roast in blackface, where he delivered a monologue of remarkably raunchy and racist humor that offended those in attendance and became major news for days. Letterman extracted a few pints of blood and laughs at Danson's expense.

Coming on the show and letting that subject be discussed was certainly a big risk, and I'd guess that Ted was fully aware of the risk of coming away looking like a buffoon or worse. But he took the risk, dealt with the matter, and, I think, came across as a decent, affable guy who used really bad judgment in one instance, has a sense of humor and humility about his own situation, and can take his hits like a man. I think his stock went up as a result of that interview.

If you aren't willing to risk actions that may cause you personal, financial or other embarrassment, you aren't going to be taking much action at all. So go ahead: screw up, fall down, embarrass yourself, and do a lot of it, as quickly as you can. Learn as much as you possibly can as you go. But, whatever you do, don't let yourself be imprisoned by the fear of making mistakes.

Death Of An Actor

One of the saddest stories to come out of Hollywood years ago was the rather sordid tale of the death of a young actor named Barry Brown. He played leading roles in *Bad Company* and *Daisy Miller,* and he was an actor of unusual promise. But he had the misfortune to do his best work in movies that were, in one way or another, unsuccessful. As he found it increasingly difficult to get parts, he became depressed, began drinking heavily and behaving erratically. He was found in his home, shot thorough the head with a gun and bottle beside him, and friends theorized he had been playing Russian roulette and had not intended suicide.

Barry Brown, dead at 27, had talent, looks and intelligence. All he lacked was the one quality that, if absent, can make the rest useless: he lacked the ability to hang in, the emotional strength necessary to 'reject rejection' and keep coming back for more.

It is the same in many professions, of course. "From salesman to saxophonist, the individual who risks something of himself in performance has to be somewhat inured to rebuff.

So wrote Bruce Cook, contributing editor to *American Film Magazine,* in an article for *The Wall Street Journal* years ago, "This story is all the more tragic when you consider that it must be representative of tens of thousands of similar stories, some reported, some not, of people who gave up."

It's such stories that prove that talent, genius, and education are no assurances of success. In fact, the history of American business is full of stories of people lacking in those qualities but strong in persistence who have achieved the incredible.

One has to wonder how much greater America would be as a nation, in all respects, if the best and the brightest were also the most persistent.

Probably the best thing about being in business for yourself is that there isn't anybody to give a letter of resignation to when the going gets tough. Industrialist C.F. Kettering said, "No one ever would have crossed the ocean if he could have gotten off the ship in the storm."

I can think of a number of times when I've wanted to quit and didn't, mostly because I couldn't. In my experience, far more business success comes purely from persistence than from invention or investment. There's a lot to be said for simply not giving up.

(Note: Portions of the above reprinted from the book *"Kennedy On Money/Business/Success,* © 1985.)

So, How *DO* You Convert Failure to Success?

First, just by hanging in. Quite often, failure transforms itself to success purely as a result of persistence. Ernest Hemingway reportedly rewrote the *Old Man And The Sea* two hundred times and tried forty-four different endings for *A Farewell To Arms.* Keep trying a slightly different approach. But keep trying.

The insightful writer Ben Stein says, "Failure is like a patient teacher who tells us, "No, THAT won't work. Try it a little differently. Or maybe a lot differently." If you look at failure as a coach, as a manager encouraging you to try different approaches, you get a much better idea of what failure is."

Second, by diligently looking for the concealed opportunity. To quote proverbs and adages: nothing is either as good or as bad as it fist appears to be... and... whenever one door closes, another opens. Personally, every great disaster, disappointment and tragedy in my life has directly led to a greater opportunity or benefit. Every single time. But, you can only find what you look for, see what you expect to see.

Are there exceptions? I suppose so. There ARE some "failures" in which I've been unable to uncover any IMMEDIATE benefit or opportunity – and those, set aside as "unfinished business" (rather than "*permanent failure*") have, in time, yielded enormous value. But these exceptions are few and far between.

Third, by taking prompt, decisive, constructive action. *Stopping* is the absolute worst thing that you can do. I wonder how many shots Michael Jordan MISSED (failures!) in his pro basketball career? Even how many CRUCIAL shots he missed? Well, one thing's certain; when he did miss one, he didn't rush over to the bench, get the coach to take him out of the game, sit down on the bench, put a towel over his head, and refuse to take another shot for the rest of the game. What did he do when he missed? As soon as possible, he took another shot.

Cotton Fitzsimmons, a wise, veteran coach once with the Phoenix Suns organization says: "Sometimes you have to let a player just shoot his way out of a slump." No, *stopping* is not the answer. Instead, as with most problems, action is the only true antidote.

- Dan Kennedy

We've Reserved A Special Gift For <u>YOU</u> From Dan Kennedy, Valued At $633.91, For Getting This Far In *The Ultimate Success Secret* (Most Don't)

GKIC.

THE

MOST INCREDIBLE Free Gift EVER

How To Claim Your $633.91 Worth of MoneyMaking Information

To Claim It Visit:

<u>www.GKICFreeGift.com</u>

CHAPTER 16

BONUS CHAPTER

UNLOCKING THE 3 NEW LAWS OF SELLING IN THE NEW ECONOMY

By Andrew J. Cass

As mentioned earlier, as I write this I'm entering my 17th year in the business of commission-only Direct Sales. In all that time, I have not ever been given a company paycheck (w-2) and I've supported myself *selling* for almost <u>two decades</u>. Twice in that time frame, in two separate businesses, I cracked the 7-figure mark, before the age of 35. Very few can say the same.

What many don't fully comprehend is that Direct Sales is when a business owner or entrepreneur sells *'direct to the consumer.'* No middle man, no one in between, no company to company (B2B) sale. Just you and the prospect. That is truly Direct Selling. Good chance your business is a Direct Selling business, regardless of the product or service you offer, and regardless of the business model and the type of business you are in.

However, the thought of *'selling'* to most business owners and entrepreneurs is sort of an uncomfortable feeling. No one *really* wants to be in sales, right? And as a result, selling becomes an afterthought and is usually not done very systematically or even with any real plan (key words: *system* and *plan*).

Furthermore, most try to sell too fast. They usually launch right into a conversation about their products and services without much thought given to *who* they are attempting to sell to. This causes an immediate *disconnect* between you and your prospect. What follows, is *resistance*. Which brings me to this critical "3-step formula" that, when deployed, will create an '*on-ramp*' to more sales for your business with very little resistance. Guaranteed.

As I like to say: "*nothing happens in business until something is sold.*" Now, let's make something happen...

Step 1 - Your Message: This is *what* you are communicating to the marketplace. This is, literally, your business's first impression. And as you know, you don't get a second chance to make a first impression.

What exactly are you communicating to the marketplace? What makes you and your product or service *unique*? What is your Unique Selling Proposition (USP)? – This something we talk A LOT about in the Renegade South Florida Entrepreneur / GKIC world.

Most have no clue or haven't given the primary message of their business much thought at all. Big mistake. Especially today, with distractions at an all-time high, where we have to fight like never before to get noticed, even for a few moments...

So here's the Million-Dollars question, invented in 1979 and copyright protected by Dan Kennedy:

"Why should I (your prospective customer, client, patient) choose to do business with you vs. any and every option available to me?"

A great question. And one you should strive to have a great answer for. Having a strong, clear, sharp answer to this question, can revolutionize your business. It did so for Dominos Pizza, a once struggling little pizza delivery company who became a publicly traded giant pizza company on the heels of this message: *"fresh, hot pizza delivered in 30-minutes or less. Guaranteed."*

How could you ever attempt to sell anything without having a clear message?

Short answer: you can't.

Step 2 - Your Market: The great majority of advertising and marketing done by businesses and entrepreneurs, at just about every level, is NOT focused on anyone. It's focused on *everyone*. As I mentioned a moment ago, this creates an immediate disconnect between you and your prospect. That's a tough place to start your sales process from, isn't it? Yet, the great majority start from this place everyday. And, naturally, they are met with great resistance.

What group of people are the best fit for your product or service? *Who* are you and your product or service for? *Who* do you stand for? *Who* has *already* expressed interest in your category?

When you have answers to these questions, you can then craft a much more targeted, clear, and relevant message to an audience, which will allow you to "connect" right off the bat. And it's this *'connection component'* early on that will be the game-changer for you and will, literally, set up the sale later on. This is known as a 'who-strategy.' Most miss this.

Remember, when you are not for *anyone*, you are for *everyone*, and your message will be immediately dismissed and diluted in an already messy marketplace.

How could you ever attempt to sell anything without knowing _who_ your market is?

Short answer: you can't.

Step 3 -Your Media: This is essentially they type of advertising you use to deliver your message: online or offline, it makes no difference - radio, TV, direct mail, pay-per-click, print (magazines, newspapers), etc. Clearly, nowadays, we have more options than ever. And that's good news and bad news...

Good news, because we have many choices that didn't exist years ago. Bad news, because all these choices can cause great confusion and overwhelm and lead us down some long, dark, dead-end roads. I see this all too often. The great majority of business owners and entrepreneurs lean toward picking the Media first, then they go back and try to figure out a Message and a Market. That's backwards. And costly. That's like trying to build a house with the walls and the windows first, then going back to add the foundation.

What if a large portion of the audience you are trying to attract mainly responds to online social media advertising but you are pouring all of your time and energy into offline magazine advertising? Or, imagine you are trying to reach a group of doctors for your product or service and you set up a pay-per-click advertising campaign for the first page of Google, but the doctors don't ever go online to search for it. However, they could easily be moved to respond had they received mail from you at their office. You get the point.

How could you ever attempt to sell anything without knowing <u>which</u> form of media your market actually responds to?

Short answer: you can't.

You will never know which *Media* your audience responds to if you do not first know <u>who</u> they are. And your *Message* will never resonate with anyone if you haven't carefully chosen <u>who</u> your *Market* is to receive it. As you can see, this formula was designed to be executed in *exact* order from step 1 to 3.

(You'll learn more about this "Message – Market – Media" formula, which will be a game-changer for your business, by attending one of our events and being involved in our local Renegade South Florida Entrepreneurs / GKIC group.)

So this begs the question...

Why do so many attempt to sell <u>without</u> a clear Message, <u>without</u> a carefully chosen Market, and <u>without</u> knowledge of the Media preferred by their target prospects?

Short answer: because they don't know what YOU just discovered here.

Selling gets easier when well prepared marketing precedes it. You might want to read that again. It does NOT work the other way around. This, in turn, makes "selling <u>more</u> with <u>less</u> resistance" a reality.

If you'd like to find out more about my trademark-protected selling system, 'The C.S.C Selling Method'™ and my 'Sales Velocity'™ Private Coaching Program, which installs this entire process into businesses, be sure to visit: <u>www.AndrewJCass.com</u> for more info.

- Andrew J. Cass

Subscribe to the Sales Velocity Podcast on iTunes by visiting: www.SalesVelocityPodcast.com

A FINAL WORD FROM DAN...

By now, you should have "locked in" on *The Ultimate Success Secret* presented to you a number of times throughout this book. The people who are LIVING this Secret are the most respected and admired, influential and powerful, successful and happy individuals on the planet.

I would like to add a very brief discussion about just one *application* of this *Secret* – and to quickly note that, like all advice, it's easier said than done; that, like "the fat doctor", I could stand to take my own medicine more frequently; but that does not diminish the importance of the ideas.

On the long, often dangerously boring drive from Phoenix to Las Vegas, there are signs posted frequently, at sites of deadly accidents, warning drivers not to drive if they've been drinking, not to drive if fatigued. The signs say:

There Is A LAST Time For Everything...

Tell your wife (or husband) you love her (or him) more often. And especially tell her (or him) *today,* because they might be gone tomorrow. There is a last time for everything.

Stop and have a friendly conversation with your Mom, Dad, a friend, the guy at the newsstand on the corner. Take just a few minutes for this more often than you do. And, especially *today*. They might be gone tomorrow. There is a last time for everything.

I called to talk to a friend the other day, another entrepreneur as busy, as obsessed as I. She wasn't in. When she called back she said, almost apologetically, and wryly, "I was out having a Life." She had gone out to lunch with someone 100% unrelated to her business. Whatever it is that you really, really enjoy doing, really, really, really enjoy it the next time you do it. There is a last time for everything.

When you go to your place of business today, be thankful you've got one, and give it the very best you've got. Tomorrow, thousands will lose their jobs – and *then,* maybe, wish they'd done things there differently. Tomorrow, a thousand entrepreneurs will close business' doors --- and *then,* maybe, wonder what might have happened if they'd advertised more creatively, sold more aggressively. There is a last time for everything.

Whatever you're going to do today, give it your best, and take from it the best you can because...

- Dan Kennedy

NOT THE END, BUT THE BEGINNING...

Now that you know "ACTION" is <u>The</u> Ultimate Success Secret, here's a somewhat funny, yet instructive saying I'll leave you with:

"Even a hungry cat won't pounce on a still mouse."

Movement is magnetic. *Action* is attractive. Yet, so many miss this. But not you. Not after reading this book. I trust you enjoyed it.

I once heard Dan Kennedy say: "The difference *is* the difference. And if you want more... a different, better, more prestigious business / life experience, you need to embrace just about everything *differently*. Differently than your peers and friends in the business. Differently than you've always done them."

I couldn't agree more. And if *YOU* agree there's more out there <u>for</u> <u>you</u>... a *different*, better, more prestigious business / life experience, then I'd like to introduce you to "The Place For Prosperity."

In chapter 12, I said, "there is NO greater power than 'the power of people' and the power of your relationships - <u>your</u> <u>Association</u>." Renegade South Florida Entrepreneurs is the fastest growing business growth group in South Florida, in partnership with GKIC, the largest *Association* of independent business owners, entrepreneurs, and sales professionals with a shared, strong interest in exceptionally effective, <u>results</u> <u>driven</u> marketing strategies. No group of people like <u>this</u> exists anywhere else in the United States.

But this "Place For Prosperity" means more than money. We are about creating and possessing skills of empowerment. We are up to something here a whole lot more significant than just some marketing strategies that make some money...

If you truly have the courage and the drive to be *different*, if you dare to be great(er), then consider this an invitation from me to you, to join us at one of our upcoming Renegade South Florida Entrepreneur / GKIC Miami Chapter events. I'd love to meet you in person. We'd love to meet you in person. For more info and location details visit: www.NoBSMiami.com

To your continued success...

- Andrew J. Cass

*I wanted to sculpt the 'Doer', but he
kept getting up to go somewhere.*

Subscribe To The Renegade South Florida Entrepreneur iPad Magazine By Visiting: www.RenegadeSFEMag.com

ABOUT THE AUTHOR – DAN KENNEDY

Dan Kennedy is the author of numerous other books, including those in the popular No B.S. series, as well as *The Ultimate Marketing Plan* and *Ultimate Sales Letter*. His books have been on bookstore shelves continuously for more than 15 years, translated in 5 languages, published in two dozen foreign countries, and on *the Business Week Magazine* and amazon.com bestseller lists, as well as an *Inc. Magazine* list of "100 best business books." In addition, he is the **editor of four business newsletters**, including the #1 marketing newsletter in America, the NO B.S. MARKETING LETTER (www.NoBSMiamiFreeGift.com).

He is the highest-fee freelance direct-response copywriter in America, "the brain behind" countless magazine ads, direct-mail campaigns, online marketing businesses, TV infomercials, catalogs, etc. As a consultant, he works with a small cadre of on-going private clients, only occasionally accepting a new client, however his networks of consultants, coaches and advisors work with over one million entrepreneurs and sales professionals every year.

For 20+ years, Dan was a busy, popular and prominent professional speaker, delivering over 2,000 presentations, including 9 years on the #1 seminar tour, appearing repeatedly with three former U.S. Presidents, Gen. Colin Powell and Gen. Norman Schwarzkopf, top athletes and coaches, Hollywood celebrities, legendary entrepreneurs and other leading business speakers including Zig Ziglar, Brian Tracy and Tom Hopkins. Currently, he speaks several times a year at GKIC events and rarely accepts other speaking engagements.

Books by the author include:

No B.S. Direct Marketing

No B.S. Business Success In The New Economy

No B.S. Sales Success In The New Economy

No B.S. Time Management For Entrepreneurs

No B.S. Wealth Attraction In The New Economy

No B.S. Ruthless Management Of People & Profits

No B.S. Trust-Based Marketing

No B.S. Price Strategy

No B.S. Marketing To Leading-Edge Boomers & Seniors

Dan Kennedy is available for speaking engagements and consulting, schedule permitting.

You may contact him by fax at: 602-269-3113

More Information about Dan's cutting-edge training programs and newsletter publications can be found by visiting: www.GKICResourcesMiami.com

ABOUT THE AUTHOR – ANDREW J. CASS

Andrew J. Cass was born and raised just outside of Boston, MA and currently resides in Miami, FL. He attended Hofstra University in New York and graduated in 1995 with a degree in Business Administration (BBA) and was also a member of the NCAA Division 1 Hofstra football team. He went on to spend ten years in the Financial Services industry in both Investment Banking and Mortgage Banking prior to becoming an Internet Marketer in 2006.

A seven-figure producer in two separate Direct Sales businesses <u>before the age of 35</u>, Andrew is a nationally recognized expert and speaker on the topics of Direct Response Marketing and Direct Sales training. He is the founder and publisher of the first-ever iPad Magazine (iMag) on the topic of 'selling', now featured on the Apple Newsstand, "Direct Selling Insider" Magazine, and is host of his own Podcast program, "Sales Velocity."

Andrew currently owns his own direct sales company in the Mobile Marketing space, RemarkaMobile. He is the Director of the Renegade South Florida Entrepreneurs group, in partnership with the GKIC and Founder & Publisher of Renegade South Florida Entrepreneur Magazine.

Having generated hundreds of thousands of leads online and Millions of dollars in sales revenue as a result, Andrew J. Cass specializes in working directly with select small business owners on building a powerful, multi-media sales process for their business.

He is available for private consulting and speaking engagements along with tele-seminar and/or webinar appearances, schedule permitting. For information, visit: www.AndrewJCass.com

You may contact Andrew at: Andrew@AndrewJCass.com
or by office phone at: (305) 359-5986

ABOUT THE CO-AUTHORS

RJon Robins:

Attorney RJon Robins champions the cause for the owners of single-shareholder small law firms who know that for a law firm to be of "service" to its clients and the community, the business must first be of service to its owner. His company, *How To MANAGE a Small Law Firm.com* provides A Safe Place for its tribe of more than 1,000 like-minded lawyers from three different countries, where they can engage in an open & unapologetic dialogue about their goals, ambitions and celebrate their successes. It is the express mission of this tribe of happy lawyers to expose and then to CRUSH 'The Doctrine of Sacrifice' which has infected their legal industry and takes all the joy and honor out of being a lawyer.

Their goal is "to liberate our brethren and inspire future generations of ambitious lawyers who should never know what it's like to feel like an outcast for embracing the desire to have a successful law firm which serves our financial, personal and professional goals and aspirations." Early in his career, after learning the hard way in his own solo law firm, about all the things lawyers don't learn in law school about the business of starting, marketing & managing a successful law firm, RJon was in the right place at the right time. In 1999 he was recognized, recruited and trained by the legendary solo & small law firm management authority, J.R. Phelps Founding Director of the first State Bar Law Office Management Assistance Service program.

As a LOMAS Practice Management Advisor it is documented that RJon had the unique opportunity to help more than one thousand lawyers and professional legal administrators with virtually every small law firm management & marketing issue conceivable. Microsoft shares RJon's commitment today to the success of solo and small law firms everywhere and acts as lead sponsor for his National Solo & Small Law Firm Success Tour which in 2011 is scheduled to conduct continuing legal education workshops in more than 15 cities nationwide (www.National-CLE-Tour).

Visit: www.HowToManageASmallLawFirm.com

Carlos Castellanos:

Carlos is an award winning illustrator/syndicated cartoonist and entrepreneur. He is the co-creator and artist behind the popular nationally syndicated newspaper comic strip 'BALDO', the most widely distributed Latino family comic strip appearing in over 250 daily and Sunday newspapers and read by millions nation wide. As the author of two books *The Lower You Ride, The Cooler You Are* and *Night of the Bilingual Telemarketers* and executive producer of the 'Baldo' Animated TV series, he now mentors and coaches other freelance artists on the secrets to earning a great income and an enviable lifestyle, doing meaningful creative work that inspires them. Additionally, he helps businesses generate more sales and leads through the use of custom designed cartoon characters and stories to instantly add personality to your marketing and create emotional connections with your audience that get you noticed and sell more of your products or services.

Visit: www.CarlosCastellanos.com/bonus

Mande White:

Mande Mande created her first information product in 2001 and has since spent the last 10 years behind the scenes of some of the most successful Internet Marketers advising on strategy, product offerings, traffic methods and conversion techniques. She has helped generate over 10,000,000 leads resulting in over $20 million is additional revenue for her clients since 2001.

Mande makes money 24/7/365 from the information products she has created in her "Magic Bullet" series including: LinkedIn Magic Bullet, Income Magic Bullet, Facebook Magic Bullet, and over a dozen more! You can find out about all her products and programs at: www.MandeWhite.com

You can request a FREE copy of her Marketing Magic Bullet program (a $297 value) by visiting: www.FreeGiftFromMande.com/UltimateSuccess

Dwight Woods:

Dwight Woods, aka: "The Jeet Kune Do Rebel," a 39 year veteran of the martial arts, is the Chief Instructor of Unified Martial Art Academy, one of Miami's oldest martial arts schools and the only school in Miami-Dade County that specializes in teaching Jeet Kune Do, the martial art and philosophy of the late martial art legend, Bruce Lee. Jeet Kune Do is a method that places an equal emphasis on using fighting skills to develop and maintain high levels of fitness and self-defense ability as well as using unique methods to develop emotional, mental and spiritual well-being. Dwight is also an in-demand coach and consultant mainly for the martial art industry but has recently delved into marketing consulting for small businesses.

Visit: www.TheJeetKuneDoRebel.com

Alle van Calker:

Alle van Calker is the owner and president of Sunvalley Solutions Inc. - "Sampling Solutions Made Easy, By Digging a Little Deeper for You." Representing the world famous Eijkelkamp Agrisearch Equipment BV from the Netherlands, SDEC from France and Umwelt Geraete Technik from Germany, we are pleased make a complete line of high quality products available for research in Soil, Water and Groundwater. Soil drilling and sampling (disturbed and undisturbed); sediment sampling; In-situ soil physical research; Soil physical research in the lab; Soil Water retention curve; Deep core samplers; Hand Auger Equipment; Percussion Drilling Equipment; Infiltration equipment, Permeameter, Penetrometers; Core samplers; Sediment samplers and more!

Visit: www.sunvalleysolutions.com or call 305-677-3325.

Debbie Wysocki:

Debbie Wysocki, aka the Network Marketing Queen, is the owner of *Women with Dreams* and *Residual Money Secrets* – companies that empower the average person to live an extraordinary life by teaching how to build profitable businesses in network marketing. She is a wife, mom, author, wellness educator, volunteer, real estate investor, and a former Beverly Hills Financial Analyst, and now a top producer & trainer in the MLM industry, who is passionate about helping others to succeed. Her motto is 'How you do anything, is how you do everything!'

Visit: www.WomenWithDreamsMLMAcademy.com

Christine Myers:

Christine Myers is the owner of *Virtual Assistant Services* based in Broward County, Florida. Before opening her own business, she was an in-house Administrative Assistant for a financial planning firm in Fort Lauderdale, Florida. In that position, she managed over 1,000 client accounts, coordinated seminar events, scheduled appointments and prepared flyers and newsletters for ad campaigns.

Christine is a graduate of VATrainer.com and the South Florida Business Institute. Through her company, *Virtual Assistant Services*, she offers administrative support to any business owner who doesn't want or doesn't need to hire a full or part-time employee, yet still needs the extra assistance to accomplish the overwhelming administrative tasks necessary to effectively run a business. She is an active member of several women's business organizations and is a board member of a local Chamber of Commerce. She also is Chairperson of a leads group through the same Chamber of Commerce and she is the Membership Coordinator for the Renegade South Florida Entrepreneurs / GKIC Miami Chapter.

To find out more about Christine and the administrative services she specializes in, visit www.VirtualAssistantServices.net.

John Tate:

John's After graduating from The Ohio State University with a Bachelor of Science in Industrial and Systems Engineering, John began his career with a large global accounting and consulting firm in its IT Management Consulting division. During the next 10 years John gained executive positions at four different companies in primarily sales and marketing roles.

During this time, the entrepreneur in John broke loose and he went on to found five small businesses. Products John has developed and marketed have been featured on QVC, The New York Times, Popular Science and Oprah's O-List.

Understanding the value of public relations and seeing first-hand the results that can be had by capturing the attention of those searching online for a product or service, John co-founded PR Machine - a hybrid PR firm that combines the best of traditional PR with Internet marketing activities that drive new business. To learn more about PR Machine visit: www.prmachine.co

*Cartoons Provided By Co-Author Carlos
Castellanos at:*

www.DrawnBySuccess.com/bonus

43182347R00130

Made in the USA
Charleston, SC
20 June 2015